Frantz Fanon

# OHIO SHORT HISTORIES OF AFRICA

This series of Ohio Short Histories of Africa is meant for those who are looking for a brief but lively introduction to a wide range of topics in African history, politics, and biography, written by some of the leading experts in their fields.

# Frantz Fanon

*Toward a Revolutionary Humanism*

Christopher J. Lee

OHIO UNIVERSITY PRESS

ATHENS

Ohio University Press, Athens, Ohio 45701
ohioswallow.com
© 2015 by Ohio University Press
All rights reserved

Printed in the United States of America
Ohio University Press books are printed on acid-free paper ⊗™

Cover design by Joey Hi-Fi

25 24 23 22 21 20 19 18 17 16 15      5 4 3 2 1

ISBN: 978-0-8214-2174-1
e-ISBN: 978-0-8214-4535-8

*Library of Congress Cataloging-in-Publication Data available.*

Names: Lee, Christopher J.
Title: Frantz Fanon : toward a revolutionary humanism / Christopher
J. Lee.
Description: Athens, Ohio : Ohio University Press, [2015] | Series:
    Ohio short histories of Africa | Includes bibliographical references
    and index.
Identifiers: LCCN 2015030650| ISBN 9780821421741 (pb : alk. paper) |
    ISBN9780821445358 (pdf)
Subjects: LCSH: Fanon, Frantz, 1925–1961—Political and social views.
    | Humanism. | Africa—Colonial influence.
Classification: LCC JC273.F36 L44 2015 | DDC 320.01—dc23
LC record available at http://lccn.loc.gov/2015030650

*This book is for*

Michael Brown Jr. (1996–2014)
Amadou Diallo (1976–1999)
Eric Garner (1970–2014)
Oscar Grant III (1986–2009)
Trayvon Martin (1995–2012)
Tamir Rice (2002–2014)

# Contents

# Illustrations

**Figures**

**Maps**

# Preface

No pedagogy which is truly liberating can remain
distinct from the oppressed by treating them as
unfortunates and by presenting for their emulation
models from among the oppressors. The oppressed
must be their own example in the struggle for their
redemption.

—Paulo Freire, *Pedagogy of the Oppressed*
(1970)[1]

I first read Frantz Fanon in Gaborone, Botswana, when
I was twenty-two. At the time my nascent professional
ambitions had centered on ecology and environmental
studies. Though I had heard Fanon's name before, this
period was the first occasion that I engaged his work
seriously. I still have the used copy of *The Wretched of
the Earth* I borrowed (and never returned), and, quite
honestly, it gave the impression of being dated at the
time. Reading it in southern, as opposed to north, Africa made its politics appear geographically distant. Its
fervor for decolonization and Third World revolution
seemed displaced after the end of the Cold War.

This initial impression soon transformed into a striking realization. A short distance away, South Africa was emerging from its remarkable democratic transition, only eighteen months into the postapartheid period. With Botswana a key frontline state during the antiapartheid struggle, Gaborone had been a base of operations for the Umkhonto we Sizwe (the MK, or "Spear of the Nation")—the military wing of the African National Congress and the South African Communist Party—in addition to providing a cross-border refuge for numerous activists fleeing the violent brutality of South Africa's white minority regime during its final decades. In retrospect, I can imagine my beaten, secondhand edition of *The Wretched of the Earth* being in the possession of any number of people involved in the political struggle further south. Fanon's work had been banned by the apartheid government, but, smuggled clandestinely into the country, it inspired a generation of activists, most significantly Steve Biko and the Black Consciousness Movement, which drew from Fanon to articulate and resist the psychological oppression of racism. The ideas embedded in Fanon's writing retained an enduring vitality and mobility of influence beyond his own political circumstances during the mid-twentieth century—a recurrence of meaning that continues to the present. Indeed, since that distant time in Botswana, his work has powerfully informed two preceding book projects of my own, one portraying the rise of the Third World and the second deconstructing colonial legacies that still inhabit the present. A key incentive for pursuing this biography has been to revisit ideas that have proved so formative in my own life.

This book serves as an introduction to Fanon and, ideally, a preface for further engagement with his thought. Its primary aim is to encourage firsthand reading of his work for the uninitiated. Given the diverse breadth and sophistication of the existing secondary literature and the practical limitations of this book series, this intellectual biography does not claim comprehensiveness of factual detail or omniscience over how to interpret Fanon's writing—an impossible undertaking in this setting. Instead, it highlights key themes and, when appropriate, stresses underdeveloped ones. Inevitably, it bears the imprint of my own interpretations and thinking too. I encourage additional reading to do justice to his work and its meanings for a range of audiences.

Three features are worth mentioning at the outset. First, this book stresses a historical contextualization of Fanon's work. Without question, Fanon's reputation precedes him. Yet knowledge of his arguments is frequently based on assumption, rather than on careful reading. Indeed, Fanon's thought is far more nuanced—and pragmatic—than many of his admirers permit. Moreover, Fanon is often used as an entry point for understanding Martinique and Algeria, whereas I firmly believe the histories of Martinique and Algeria should be entry points for understanding Fanon. This empirical approach is not intended to diminish the life of his ideas. Instead, it is meant to emphasize Fanon's acute sensibility toward the world around him and his unique ability to translate its broader repercussions.

Second, unlike many existing studies, several chapters perform a basic walkthrough of his books to provide readers with a clear, if abbreviated, sense of their structure, language, argumentation, strengths, and weaknesses. This book seeks to balance Fanon's life and the voice found within his texts. This expository approach may seem prosaic, but it stands in contrast with many critical assessments that focus on particular ideas, specific essays, and even individual aphorisms, while neglecting the cul-de-sacs, the repetition, as well as the broader narrative structures that frame his analyses—in addition to the historical contexts that chronologically shaped his insights.

Third, this book draws attention to a distinct ethic found in Fanon's politics and writing—what I call radical empathy—that is touched upon in the epigraph by Paulo Freire, a Brazilian activist-intellectual deeply influenced by Fanon. Despite Fanon's privileged middleclass upbringing and elite education, his arguments are ultimately marked by persistent consideration for oppressed people and communities: identifying with their experiences, learning from their example, and using such knowledge to pursue political change. This principle of humane recognition is Fanon's most enduring lesson—one still resonant that deserves renewed notice in our politically fraught era.

A number of people helped with this project. I thank Gillian Berchowitz for her initial invitation and for her persistent editorial reassurance. Jerry Buttrey, Jeffrey Byrne, Sharad Chari, Judith Coffin, John Comaroff, Fred Cooper, Yoav Di-Capua, John Drabinski, Sarah Duff, John Gibler, Nigel Gibson, Barbara Harlow, Neville Hoad, Isabel Hofmeyr, Priya Lal, James Le Sueur, Dan Magaziner, Minkah Makalani, Kris Manjapra, Marc Matera, Achille Mbembe, Walter Mignolo, Sarah Nuttall, Philippe Peycam, David Scott, Todd Shepard, Jon Soske, Cirila Toplak, and Françoise Vergès provided answers, conversation, and comments on portions of the manuscript. I am immensely grateful. I started this project while a visiting fellow at the Institute for Historical Studies at the University of Texas at Austin. I thank its then director, Julie Hardwick, as well as Jeremi Suri for their warm support. A grant from the government of India provided financial support at the University of the Witwatersrand, Johannesburg. I completed this book while a Sheila Biddle Ford Foundation Fellow at the Hutchins Center for African and African American Research at Harvard University. I extend unqualified gratitude to Bradley Craig, Krishna Lewis, Abby Wolf, and, not least, Henry Louis Gates Jr. for time, assistance, and encouragement that proved indispensable toward the end.

Finally, a word about the dedication. This book is not a typical work of scholarship. It has been motivated by a set of political and moral convictions. While I was completing penultimate revisions, Michael Brown was killed in Ferguson, Missouri, on August 9, 2014, and the police officer who shot him, Darren Wilson, was exonerated of wrongdoing several months later, on November 24. This case is a world apart from Frantz Fanon's, and police should not be universally construed as hostile. Yet, to my mind, this tragedy speaks to the continued dehumanization of black and other racial minority communities in some quarters, and the recurrence of violence toward such communities as a result—matters that Fanon grappled with during his lifetime. I remain troubled by this situation. This book is dedicated, in this spirit, to the memory of Brown, Amadou Diallo, Eric Garner, Oscar Grant, Trayvon Martin, and Tamir Rice—a few among many.

# A Note on Translations and Editions

Frantz Fanon has been widely translated since the 1960s. Given that this text is primarily pedagogical in scope and meant to be read alongside his books, I have relied on the editions of his work most readily available in the United States and South Africa, where this book is being published jointly by two presses. Though translations by Richard Philcox are the most recent, I have also relied on earlier editions by Haakon Chevalier, Constance Farrington, and Charles Lam Markmann, due to their relative strengths and still wide availability in university and public libraries, as well as in bookstores. I have cited which editions I use in the endnotes.

Introduction

# Unthinking Fanon

*Worlds, Legacies, Politics*

> Reality, for once, requires a total understanding.
> On the objective level as on the subjective level,
> a solution has to be supplied.
> —*Black Skin, White Masks*[i]

Frantz Fanon was born in 1925 on Martinique in the French Antilles, an archipelago of islands scattered across the southeastern edge of the Caribbean between Haiti and South America. He died in 1961 from leukemia in a hospital in Bethesda, Maryland, just outside Washington, D.C. Trained as a psychiatrist, Fanon achieved fame as a political theorist of anticolonial liberation struggle. During his brief thirty-six-year life, he published two seminal books: *Black Skin, White Masks* (1952) and *The Wretched of the Earth* (1961), the latter appearing in print just days before his death. These two books addressed the psychological effects of racism and the politics of the Algerian Revolution (1954–62), respectively. He also wrote a less-appreciated third book titled *Year Five of the*

*Algerian Revolution* (1959, reprinted and translated as *A Dying Colonialism* in 1967), in addition to numerous medical journal articles and political essays both under his name and anonymously, a selection of which appeared in the posthumous collection *Toward the African Revolution* (1964). Despite the brevity of his life and written work, Fanon's observations and analysis of colonialism and decolonization in these books have remained vital, due to their firsthand immediacy as well as the incisiveness of his ideas.

Indeed, Fanon's prescient insights have influenced a range of academic fields, such that the term *Fanonism* has been invented as shorthand to capture his interrelated political, philosophical, and psychological arguments. Through penetrating views and a frequently bracing prose style, the small library of Fanon's work has become essential reading in postcolonial studies, African and African American studies, critical race theory, and the history of insurgent thought, to name just a few subjects. The secondary literature on his work continues to grow apace. Above all, Fanon remains a political martyr, who died before he could witness the birth of an independent Algeria, his stature near mythic in scale as a result. To invoke Fanon is to bring forth a radical worldview dissatisfied with the political present, reproachful of the conformities of the past, and consequently in perpetual struggle for a better future.

But who is Frantz Fanon? His diverse career, personal geography, and complex ideas defy any simplistic rendition of his life. Indeed, the wide-ranging influence of his work over the past fifty years has often prompted a rudimentary sense of his biography, with his books and essays being a substitute for the man himself. Like other writers and intellectuals, Fanon is regularly appreciated in textual terms, rather than through the facets and challenges of his own personal experience. Explaining the political orientation of the Black Panther Party, Huey P. Newton (1942–1989), one of its leaders, once declared, "We read the work of Frantz Fanon, particularly *The Wretched of the Earth*, the four volumes of Chairman Mao Tse-tung, and Che Guevara's *Guerrilla Warfare*."[2] Such is the approach that emerged shortly after Fanon's death and has since extended to the present day, with his insights still providing vital methods of political interpretation.

However, this critical application has had, at times, a seemingly incongruous effect. Edward Said (1935–2003), the esteemed Palestinian scholar, once insisted, for example, that Fanon be read alongside Jane Austen as a means of rethinking the Western canon.[3] Others have taken this textual approach even further, to the point of scripture, seeing Fanon as a near spiritual figure akin to the Indian nationalist leader Mohandas Gandhi (1869–1948).[4] Though this textual angle is understandable, given the range of Fanon's ideas and the highly personal nature of his work, it has also frequently sanctified his writing, resulting in overwrought assessments and muted debate, with sharp criticism of Fanon typically played in a minor key—a situation that lends itself to hagiography.

Grasping his life and its human limitations in detail provides a more acute sense of his ambition, the experiences that informed it, and why his books have offered continued resonance for different audiences. Henry Louis Gates Jr., a leading intellectual of African American studies, once noted the relative disregard for Fanon's personal history in contemporary scholarship, which occasioned the anachronistic use of Fanon's work that was too alienated from the specific colonial contexts and revolutionary spirit that influenced his thinking.[5] The tendency toward mythmaking surrounding Fanon has often rendered him an uncomplicated universal symbol—an emblematic, and thus ahistorical, voice against colonialism in its varied forms across time and place, without attention to the reception and meaning of his work during his lifetime.[6] When we remove him from history, we risk making him a cliché.

This book offers a historical portrait of Fanon. It is written in the belief that it is essential to understand his life experiences in order to grasp the origins of his thought and its evolution over time. Indeed, the aura of destiny presents a constant challenge. Fanon is too often treated as a fully formed thinker, without granting him a period of apprenticeship that is indispensable to any political or intellectual life. As Alice Cherki, a former colleague of his, has forcefully argued, an "unrestrained idealization" of Fanon has created a "heroic image" that "cuts him off from history."[7] But the profile offered here is not a mere recounting of facts. His writing and biography are tightly interwoven. Understanding his life and the life of his philosophy at once not only serves to address the complex sources of his ceaselessly energetic thinking—what political theorist Achille Mbembe has called his "metamorphic thought"—but also underscores dramatic shifts in perspective over the course of his youth and adulthood, the improbability of his status as a revolutionary, and the intellectual and professional restlessness that carried him from Martinique, to France, and, finally, to Africa.[8] Intellectual figures are often perceived as solitary, inhabiting a realm of thought and therefore existing primarily on the page. While textual engagement is integral to this book, understanding Fanon as a historical figure is central.

In this regard, we must unthink Fanon. We must situate him in time, beyond the shifting vicissitudes of social and political theory. Fanon was profoundly shaped by the people he encountered and the social contexts and historical period in which he lived. He assumed a number of roles: being a son, a sibling among eight children, a husband, and a father, in addition to his better-known vocations as a psychiatrist, writer, and revolutionary activist. His philosophy was drawn from interacting with unnamed Algerian patients in his capacity as a medical doctor, as well as from relationships with such esteemed intellectual figures as Aimé Césaire (1913–2008) and Jean-Paul Sartre (1905–1980). His history must also be anchored within a deeper history of slavery, colonialism, and racism in the Americas that touched his life in different ways. Fanon is part of the history of the Black

Atlantic—a world of transatlantic connections between Africa, Europe, and the Americas—as well as the intellectual milieu of mid-twentieth-century European continental philosophy. Above all, Fanon witnessed the emergence of a new world order through European decolonization and political independence in Africa and Asia, achieved through strident public criticism and violent armed struggle. Fanon occupied several political, professional, and intellectual worlds that underwent profound shifts over the course of his brief lifetime—worlds that he himself helped define.

The colonial and metropolitan settings Fanon traversed have also generated an intricate set of political and intellectual legacies that must be untangled—from the Caribbean, to Africa and the Middle East, to university settings in Europe and North America. His life presents a distinct historical problem, resisting conformity to many existing narratives of black intellectual history and the origins of revolutionary thought. David Macey, a biographer of Fanon, has written that despite the continued popularity of Fanon's books and his widespread name recognition, he remains something of an enigma, a quality that can be attributed to his contingent cosmopolitanism: from his birth and childhood in Martinique, to his military service and early career in France, to his eventual activism in Algeria and North Africa. These contrasting contexts produced a sequence of identities that were geopolitical—Martinican, French, and Algerian—as well as occupational—soldier, student, psychiatrist, writer, and diplomat. They added layers of experience that both reinforced and unraveled his sociopolitical status as a black citizen of the French Empire, as he critically examined in first book, *Black Skin, White Masks.* This wide-ranging geography has also contributed to an uneven memory of Fanon that has been romanticized, contested, and, in some locales, nearly forgotten.

In France the legacy of Fanon has largely been absent or ignored until recently, in step with a general French ambivalence toward Algeria. Representing a profound loss to France, the French government refused to call the Algerian War—known as the Algerian Revolution in Algeria—a war at all, since defining it as such would imply that Algeria was a separate territory apart from France, an idea antithetical to many French. Because of the French government's preference for classifying it as a police action until 1999, it became popularly known, particularly among critics, as the "war without a name."[9] In contrast, Fanon's intellectual contributions have been eulogized extensively within the field of postcolonial studies, as well as African American and African diasporic studies in North America. Engagement with his work by such scholars as Homi K. Bhabha, Ato Sekyi-Otu, Lewis Gordon, Nigel Gibson, and others has resulted in the canonization of *Black Skin, White Masks* and *The Wretched of the Earth* as essential works for understanding the psychological impact of colonial racism and the politics of decolonization during the twentieth century. Such assessments have created a stronger Anglophone, rather than

Francophone, tradition in Fanon studies. Indeed, there is an incongruity that Fanon's reputation has reached its apex in the American academy, given his criticism toward the United States and his premature death there—the only occasion he visited the country. A more tragic irony is that his posthumous status in Martinique is a contested one and that his memory in Algeria has greatly diminished. Algeria has moved well beyond its revolutionary period, its politics more recently defined by civil conflict since the early 1990s that has pitted the government against Islamic insurgents, leaving as many as 200,000 dead. The places that meant the most to Fanon have treated the contributions of his life either with gradual forgetfulness or disregard.

Fanon's relative obscurity in Martinique until recently has been attributed to his permanent departure from there and his eventual burial in Algeria. Regarding his compatriot's unsettled memory, the critic Édouard Glissant (1928–2011) once wrote, "It so happens that years go by without his name (not to mention his work) being mentioned by the media, whether political or cultural, revolutionary or leftist, of Martinique. An avenue in Fort-de-France is named after him. That is about it."[10] Joby Fanon has recalled that his younger brother Frantz was seen as a traitor for his radical politics against France, given that Martinique has remained a part of France to the present day.[11] But Martinique was ultimately a place of childhood. Fanon achieved his fame elsewhere. Martinican residents such as Césaire,

Glissant, and Patrick Chamoiseau (1953–present) have contributed more to the island's intellectual and political life. Albert Memmi (1920–present)—the Tunisian writer whose influential work *The Colonizer and the Colonized* (1957) is often compared with Fanon's—has suggested that Fanon developed an ambivalence toward his home, as witnessed in arguments made in *Black Skin, White Masks*.[12] At a 1978 United Nations (UN) conference held in tribute to Fanon's legacy, the intellectual C. L. R. James (1901–1989) discussed how Fanon left the Caribbean in the same way that activist George Padmore (1903–1959) and James himself had once left, believing more fervently in Africa's revolution than any political change in the Caribbean. However, James believed that Fanon would have returned.[13] Indeed, this possibility is indicated in a late essay attributed to Fanon. Titled "Blood Flows in the Antilles under French Domination" (1960), this piece compares Martinique's situation to Algeria's, with Fanon expressing the sentiment of being "violently shaken" by recent events in the place of his birth.[14]

The decline of Fanon's memory in Algeria poses equally difficult questions. One answer for this absence was his lack of a top leadership position within the anti-colonial National Liberation Front (Front de Libération Nationale or FLN) and his consequent marginalization within the pantheon of Algerian nationalists. The nature of the Algerian struggle itself stressed the role of the popular masses—one slogan being "Only one hero: the People"—over the importance of individual leaders.

Authority within the FLN was also no guarantee, as the party was wracked by internal divisions during and after the war—the untimely removal of Ahmed Ben Bella (1916–2012), Algeria's first president, in 1965 being a case in point. More significant, however, was the perception of Fanon as a foreigner in Algeria, despite his political allegiance to the FLN and his burial in the eastern part of the country. It is a view that has never diminished. Although his name marks the hospital where he once worked, as well as a school and a street in Algiers, Fanon has remained an outsider, his personal history in Algeria being fixed to a specific period. At the same 1978 UN meeting, Mohamed Bedjaoui, the Algerian ambassador to France, tacitly captured this ambiguity, saying Fanon was "still alive in our hearts" seventeen years after his death, though Bedjaoui would not "give way to the very strong temptation to claim him for Algeria, because that most certainly would narrow the scope of a man whose only frontiers were the boundaries of freedom, of justice and of dignity."[15] Fanon himself began to think beyond Algeria toward the end of his life, with *The Wretched of the Earth* outlining a broader political geography that encompassed the rest of Africa and the rising Third World. But the political language he articulated has also had, arguably, less utility and declining meaning over the past fifty years for Algerians, given its strident critique of French colonialism. The paradigms of thought that his work confronted—including Négritude and ethno-psychiatry, in addition to French racism and colonialism—appear to be a world apart for generations of Algerians born since the revolution.

This book is written against this perception of irrelevance. Following the lead of other scholars, it argues for Fanon's continued significance based on his enduring insights. He was not only a critic of colonialism but an early critic of postcolonialism, with hard-won assessments that still apply to present-day Algeria and elsewhere. This book further makes this case for Fanon's importance through the example of his life. In particular, this book stresses the form of political engagement Fanon cultivated—what I call radical empathy. Radical empathy is not an expression that he used. I introduce it in this book to reinterpret his concerns and to capture the individual, rather than national or anticolonial, politics he defined and exemplified. Indeed, Fanon ultimately declared himself Algerian, exemplifying a revolutionary transformation in his own subjectivity. But radical empathy provided a first step. As a concept and practice, it seeks to move Fanon away from textual abstraction by outlining a personal and more affective dimension to his political commitments. Grounded in his medical work and his strong identification with the Algerian struggle, it outlines a political ethic beyond the antiracism and anticolonial violence he famously promoted, though this practice of moral engagement emerged from these better-known positions. Fanon's politics were not purely contrarian. They equally sought new forms of connection and solidarity.

This approach thus not only seeks to provide an alternative understanding of his life. It intends to make him more accessible—less a myth, and more human. Since his death in 1961, Fanon's thought has influenced activists across the world, from civil rights struggles in the United States to the Black Consciousness Movement in South Africa. More recently, the Arab Spring that swept North Africa and the Middle East in 2011 recalled earlier histories of regional political dissent, of which Fanon was a vital part. Controversy over Israeli settlements in the occupied West Bank has also revived Fanonian views toward settler colonialism. Fanon presents a genealogy of twentieth-century activism different from figures like Gandhi, Martin Luther King Jr. (1929–1968), and Desmond Tutu (1931–present), each of whom espoused nonviolence as a means for achieving political change. Similar to figures like Mao Tse-tung (1893–1976), Ernesto "Che" Guevara (1928–1967), and Amílcar Cabral (1924–1973), Fanon instead advocated certain forms of violence as a political necessity, reflecting an extended period of armed struggle during the 1950s and 1960s that included the First Indochina War (1946–54) against French rule in Southeast Asia, the Mau Mau Uprising (1952–60) in British colonial Kenya, the Cuban Revolution (1953–59) led by Fidel Castro (1926–present) and Guevara, and the turn of South Africa's antiapartheid struggle to armed resistance, most notably through the Umkhonto we Sizwe (MK), a military organization founded in 1961 by the African National Congress and the South African Communist Party.

Violence remains the most controversial issue regarding Fanon—an intrinsic, yet polarizing, dimension of his work that has strengthened his critics and been an inconvenient topic for his admirers. It arguably explains the greater popularity of *Black Skin, White Masks* over *The Wretched of the Earth*—the latter outlining his argument for violent struggle. It is an issue that still deserves debate. But to mark this embrace of violence as the singular feature of Fanon's politics is too reductive. Violence remained a strategic choice. It was historically situated for Fanon—a response to the pure violence of colonialism. Armed struggle did not apply universally across time and place. Indeed, this prevalent critical perspective on Fanon, popularized by other intellectuals such as Hannah Arendt (1906–1975), often elides his experience as a psychiatrist who treated victims of torture and violence during the Algerian War.[16] Fanon did not categorically promote violence for this reason. Unlike Mao, Guevara, and Cabral, he did not pick up a gun and find a permanent place on the battlefield of revolution. Though he argued for its tactical necessity and cathartic potential, Fanon recognized its traumatic impact from firsthand experience.

His greater political legacy—still relevant today—is the form of political empathy he nurtured in Algeria and Tunisia, while active with the FLN. Fanon was neither Algerian, nor an Arab, nor a Muslim by birth. Unlike many anticolonial leaders and activists, he did not participate in a struggle located in his country of origin. His arrival in Algeria was based entirely on professional contingencies.

Fanon's identification with the Algerian struggle, however, ultimately rested with his own experience with French colonialism, the self-knowledge he gained with *Black Skin, White Masks,* and his consequent ability to empathize with the Algerian people and their situation as depicted in *A Dying Colonialism* and *The Wretched of the Earth*—despite his own experiences of discrimination by Algerians, despite class and cultural distinctions between himself and those he sought to represent, despite lack of fluency in Arabic, despite being considered a foreigner.

Josie Fanon, his wife, once said that people "have often wondered why he should have taken part in the liberation of a country which was not his originally." Her reply was that only "narrow minds and hearts" for whom race or religion "constitutes an unbridgeable gulf" fail to understand—there was no contradiction or dilemma for Fanon, only necessity.[17] Fanon achieved this kind of transcendence of identity only through the intense self-reflection that characterized his intellectual life, combined with the personal mobility and expansive geography that his life eventually encompassed, granting him a perspective he would not have attained otherwise. Yet radical empathy is not synonymous with cosmopolitanism. It is a political outcome of cosmopolitanism. It is a civic effect of his transcolonial experiences in Martinique and Algeria, as well as his postcolonial experiences in Tunisia, Morocco, Ghana, and Mali. Radical empathy is one struggled-for result of the "total understanding" Fanon sought and first identified in *Black Skin, White Masks,* as cited in the

opening epigraph. It is a mechanism for the new humanism he aspired to at the end of *The Wretched of the Earth.*
His internationalism and political evolution were firmly
interwoven.

This book therefore does not propose an uncritical
nostalgia for Fanon, renouncing the present and the future
to reclaim a mystical past, to paraphrase his own words.[18]
Instead, this short book seeks to humanize Fanon—to reclaim his life and make his work immediate, as he himself
sought. A historical approach is vital in this regard. Rather
than Fanon being an entry point for understanding the
Algerian Revolution, this book proposes the converse: the
prefatory need to understand the complexities of Algeria
in order to comprehend Fanon. Rather than resorting to
Fanon's work first to explain colonialism, decolonization,
and a once-emergent Third Worldism, the history set
forth here positions these phenomena as indispensable
for situating Fanon's ambitions. Approaching Fanon in
this manner is not meant to diminish him as simply a
product of his time. He defined his time. This historical
technique is intended to underscore his uncanny ability
to interpret the politics of the period, what was at stake,
and what needed to be done.

In like fashion, this book aims to reestablish the relevance of his life and philosophy in the political present—after the wave of global decolonization that
occurred during the twentieth century, after the end of
apartheid in South Africa, and after the Arab Spring. At a
certain level, this argument for his continued importance

is at odds with Fanon's own perspective on his life and work—a tension that emerges from time to time in his writing between fixing his ideas to a specific political horizon and casting his critical glance toward the future. "In no way is it up to me to prepare for the world coming after me," he writes at one point in *Black Skin, White Masks*. "I am resolutely a man of my time."[19] In calling for a continuation of Fanon's legacy, this book reflects this need for balance—for addressing and adhering to historical specificity, while also emulating Fanon's own intellectual and political aspirations that were in constant search for solutions, to realize a better world.

# 1

# Martinique

> There were some who wanted to equate me
> with my ancestors, enslaved and lynched: I
> decided that I would accept this.
> —*Black Skin, White Masks*[1]

Frantz Fanon was born in Fort-de-France, the capital of
Martinique, on July 20, 1925. Martinique is often a cipher
in many studies of Fanon, treated merely as a place of
origin. But its deep history fundamentally informed his
identity and shaped his ambitions. A small island of approximately 1,128 square kilometers (436 square miles)
located toward the southern reaches of the Lesser Antilles
near South America (see map 1.1), Martinique's size and
geography suggest a peripheral status within the French
Empire. However, contrary to these surface qualities, the
island experienced the firm entrenchment of French rule
and influence beginning in the seventeenth century. Local
indigenous societies were quickly subsumed through
conquest, with European settler and enslaved African
communities defining Martinique's political and cultural life. French control took hold in a way that reflected

Map 1.1 The Antilles and the Caribbean.

metropolitan concerns for maintaining authority and legitimacy in a geographically distant, yet economically important, territory.

These long-standing conditions elucidate the complex search for political and cultural alternatives by figures like Fanon, Aimé Césaire, and Édouard Glissant, generating a particular Antillean discourse (*discours antillais*), to invoke an expression of Glissant's.[2] Martinique remains a part of France to the present day—an overseas department (*département d'outre-mer*) like Guiana in South America, Mayotte and Réunion in the Indian Ocean, and Guadeloupe, also in the Caribbean. Indeed, it is a historical irony that Césaire and Fanon, as vocal critics of colonialism, originated from a place that did not ultimately achieve independence like other French territories in the Americas, Africa, and Asia. Still, this basic fact and the deep-seated French-ness in Martinique also explain their motivations, underlining how and why such a small place produced vital thinkers who confronted the paradox of French rule that promised political and social equality in principle, but denied it in practice. Racism, based on a history of black enslavement, underpinned this contradiction.

## Slavery and Its Enduring Legacies

As with many European colonies, the French acquisition of Martinique was prompted by competition with other imperial powers, as well as its economic potential. Originally occupied by indigenous Arawak and Carib communities, Martinique was identified and mapped by Christopher Columbus (1451–1506) in 1493. France claimed it almost 150 years later in September 1635, when a group of French settlers established Saint-Pierre (or St. Pierre), having been pushed off the neighboring island of St. Kitts by the British. But Martinique's political status remained uncertain during the next two centuries, with the British occupying the island on several occasions. Only after the Napoleonic Wars (1803–15) did French rule stabilize, lasting to the present day. Still, by the early eighteenth century, slavery had been established within the island's economy, following the 1685 promulgation of the *Code noir*—the French legal decree by King Louis XIV (1638–1715) that formalized slavery and restricted the freedom of emancipated blacks. Coffee and especially sugar became the key commodities produced by slaves for export to Europe—an extremely lucrative trade, such that France gave up its sizeable Canadian possessions (including present-day Quebec and Ontario) at the end of the Seven Years' War (1756–63) against the British, in order to retain the far smaller territories of Martinique and Guadeloupe.

Though Fanon was born well after abolition, the history of slavery on Martinique is vital to understanding his personal origins, the racism he fought against, as well as the anticipatory role that slave emancipation had for ideas of anticolonial liberation. Enslavement incurred a form of social death, to use sociologist Orlando Patterson's expression, which left enduring legacies of dehumanization and lower-strata status.[3] The practice of slavery on Martinique took the particularly harsh form that characterized sugar production across the Caribbean. Its brutality would have lasting political, economic, and intellectual effects. First introduced to the Western Hemisphere by Columbus, sugar cultivation spread around the Caribbean over the next several centuries, sparking economic growth across the Atlantic world. Indeed, as argued by scholar-politician Eric Williams (1911–1981), this commodity generated enough surplus wealth to help initiate the Industrial Revolution in Europe during the nineteenth century.[4] The triangle trade that sent slaving ships from Europe to West and Central Africa, slaves from Africa to the Western Hemisphere, and sugar and other slave-produced commodities—such as cotton, tobacco, and coffee—to Europe created a cycle of commerce that altered European consumer tastes, encouraged imperial expansion, and transformed the political histories of many African states, which both participated in and fell victim to the slave trade. No less significant, it fundamentally changed the demography of the Americas, bringing millions of African people north and south of the equator. African slaves in turn profoundly shaped the economies, cultures, and politics of the Western Hemisphere. But they did so in the wake of the Middle Passage—the westward journey of slave ships across the Atlantic—during which millions died from disease, malnutrition, and physical mistreatment.

Violence and mortality continued to define the lives of those who arrived. The presence of death in its spectral and actual forms circumscribed the lifeworlds of those enslaved. Disease and the threat of corporal punishment caused constant anxiety. The backbreaking nature of cultivating, harvesting, and processing sugarcane weakened physical regimens and shortened the lifespans of many. Practices of commemoration subsequently emerged that sought to preserve cultural tradition and senses of African identity, in order to resist the overwhelming nature of enslavement, geographic dislocation, and colonial disempowerment.[5] These customs also insured that slavery and its violent history would never be forgotten in popular memory. Although the abolition of slavery in Martinique in 1848—coincidentally, the same year France claimed control over the territory of Algeria—preceded Fanon's birth by almost eighty years, the legacy of slavery and its dehumanization continued to ripple up through the twentieth century, marking Fanon's history and social status as it did for so many other black men and women in Martinique and throughout the Americas. Fanon never addressed slavery in his own writing with the same rigor as other topics.[6] But its pervasive latency in Martinican society unquestionably informed his political outlook, as indicated by the epigraph for this chapter.

Balancing this history of racial oppression was an overlapping history of rebellion. The French Revolution (1789–99) affected the Caribbean, with the Haitian Revolution (1791–1804) being the most significant political outcome in the region—a world-shattering revolt led by Toussaint L'Ouverture (1743–1803) along with other former and rebel slaves, who embraced the rights of liberty, equality, and fraternity as espoused by the Declaration of the Rights of Man and Citizen (1789). The meaning of the Haitian Revolution should not be underestimated. Not only did it signify the global reach of the French Revolution, but it vividly underscored the capacity of African slaves to resist their bondage and establish a new political order, to the shock and fear of slave owners throughout the Western Hemisphere. The Haitian Revolution remains the only slave revolt in history to result in the founding of a new sovereign state. This overwhelming fact generated immediate anxieties that similar uprisings could be staged north in the United States and south in Latin America. But the meaning of Haiti has equally extended to the twentieth century, becoming an early symbol of anticolonial revolution as argued by the Trinidadian intellectual C. L. R. James.[7] For Martinique, the French Revolution resulted in citizenship rights being extended to persons of color, with slavery itself abolished in 1794. However, a British takeover of the island the same year and the Napoleonic Wars prolonged slavery's slow death until 1848. Nevertheless, Martinique, similar to Haiti, experienced tension and debate over slavery and citizenship rights. This regional political tradition of resistance informed the views of Martinicans.[8]

Yet, unlike Haiti, the end of slavery in Martinique did not spell the end of colonial rule. It did grant legal citizenship rights to the island's inhabitants—Fanon was a French citizen by birth. But this political failure and the continuities between enslavement and colonialism were not overlooked by Martinique's intellectuals, including Fanon. In *Black Skin, White Masks,* he deftly insinuates this perspective, writing, "I am not the slave of the Slavery that dehumanized my ancestors."[9] Fanon instead felt indentured by his racial status and the cultural chauvinism he faced under French colonial control. This prejudice was both local and imperial in its dimensions. The basic structure of inequality in Martinique along lines of race and class was forged in the crucible of slavery and continued up through the early twentieth century—a hierarchy reinforced by demographic numbers and white political and economic control.

The population of slaves in 1696—roughly a decade after the *Code noir* decree—approximated 13,126 people out of a total population of 20,066. By the time of emancipation in 1848, slaves numbered 67,447 people out of an overall population of 120,357.[10] Slaves therefore remained in the majority for more than 150 years. But while these figures indicate a stable population ratio over time, they do not reflect the full magnitude of racial difference on the island. Many of those in the nonslave minority were also of African descent, either as freed slaves or *gens de couleur libres* ("free people of color"), a group principally comprised of *métis* (persons of multiracial background) born from relationships between European men and slave women. Though tensions of race and status emerged between these different groups, an overwhelming nonwhite majority existed, persisting to the present. Approximately 90 percent of Martinique's population today is of African descent.

This racial demography combined with the social hierarchy that slavery and colonialism constructed—with a white minority occupying the top tier—set the stage for Fanon's worldview: a perspective defined by belonging to a majority, yet one unjustly limited by racial discrimination. Landownership stayed in the hands of a ruling white plantation class after emancipation. Labor continued to be provided by black Martinicans, augmented by indentured immigrants from India, primarily Tamils from French-controlled Pondicherry. As a result, political power remained among elite whites and *békés*—Creole whites who descended from the original French settler community.[11]

## Middle-Class Life in Fort-de-France

The recorded history of the Fanon family starts in the 1840s with his great-grandfather, who was the son of a slave but himself a free man. Fanon's great-grandparents and grandparents owned small farms. His parents, Félix Casimir Fanon (1891–1947) and Eléanore Médélice Fanon (1891–1981), lived in urban Fort-de-France, working as a civil servant and shopkeeper, respectively (map 1.2). They had eight children, Frantz being the fifth. His mother was *métisse*—which may have granted Fanon some status, due to Martinique's racial politics— with part of her family being from Strasbourg in the Alsace region along the border of Germany and France. The Germanic name "Frantz" is understood to be a gesture toward this familial past. Given the professional occupations of his parents, Fanon was born into relative privilege—a first-generation, middle-class milieu—even if the degree of affluence possible in Fort-de-France at the time was limited.[12]

The population of Fort-de-France approximated 43,000 people during the 1930s, a decade after Fanon's birth, signaling the small scale of its economy and urban life generally. While it maintained all the essentials of a Caribbean port city with commercial facilities and a French naval installation, business activity was minimal and largely local after the decline of sugar's profitability at the end of the nineteenth century. Fort-de-France had long been Martinique's center of government, but

Map 1.2 Martinique.

the historical and cultural hub of the island had been its
first settlement, Saint-Pierre, once known as "the Paris of
the Caribbean." Saint-Pierre experienced a cataclysmic
downfall in 1902 with the volcanic eruption of Mount
Pelée that emitted a cloud of toxic gas, killing 30,000
people in its wake. Fort-de-France consequently swelled
in size in the decades that followed. Urbanization delivered a mix of benefits and drawbacks. The promise of
work and financial opportunity for Martinicans without
land competed with everyday problems of poor living

conditions, inadequate sanitation, and disease due to an expanding urban population. Smallpox, leprosy, and tuberculosis were common.[13]

Fanon himself escaped the worst of these conditions. His family accrued enough wealth for household servants, private schooling, and a second home. Fanon never wrote about or discussed this relative affluence. Indeed, Alice Cherki, in her memoir of Fanon, recalls his persistent privacy, writing, "Every time Jean-Paul Sartre wanted to know some particular concerning Fanon's life, Fanon avoided answering by dismissing the information as extraneous."[14] Though Sartre, as a strong admirer of Fanon, was undoubtedly interested in the origins of his philosophy, Fanon's youth sharply contrasted with the lives of those he advocated later in his adulthood, particularly in *The Wretched of the Earth.* Fanon was not an organic intellectual in the Gramscian sense, emerging from a lower-strata milieu.[15] He instead grew up in comfort with his attention focused on school, sports, and play. His family was not overtly political and, from a cultural outlook, French. Though his father maintained a certain distance from his children, Eléanore was an active presence, cultivating a rich family life. Fanon played soccer and frequented the local public library—the Bibliothèque Schœlcher—as a teenager. Joby Fanon, his older brother, recalled him being something of a mischievous trouble-maker—a quality that portended of his future, as well as undermining a common caricature of Fanon as the angry man, humorless in disposition.[16] Most significant,

Frantz Fanon attended private school at the Lycée Victor Schœlcher—which, like the library, was named after the famous French abolitionist—where, as a student, he fortuitously crossed paths with Martinican poet, intellectual, and politician Aimé Césaire.[17]

Césaire was born in 1913 in Basse-Pointe to the far north of the island. His family moved to Fort-de-France after he himself received a scholarship to study at the Lycée Schœlcher. Raised in lower middle-class circumstances—his father a government worker, his mother a seamstress—Césaire excelled academically like the younger Fanon, receiving a second scholarship to attend the Lycée Louis-le-Grand in Paris in 1934 and later the École Normale Supérieure—among the most prestigious institutions of higher learning in France. Founded during the French Revolution in 1794, it graduated such esteemed intellectual figures as Sartre, philosopher Louis Althusser (1918–1990), sociologist Pierre Bourdieu (1930–2002), and philosopher Jacques Derrida (1930–2004), among many others. After completing a master's thesis, Césaire returned to Martinique to teach. During his brief four-year tenure at the Lycée Schœlcher, Césaire taught not only Fanon but also Glissant, who credited Césaire as being a teacher of influence by assigning texts by the poet Arthur Rimbaud (1854–1891) and the novelist André Malraux (1901–1976), whose work introduced interrelated questions of aesthetics and politics.[18]

Nevertheless, these personal connections were delicate. Although Césaire and Fanon would always share a special affinity—Césaire would later write a eulogy for Fanon in the journal *Présence africaine*—generational and political differences emerged, as seen in *Black Skin, White Masks,* perhaps an unsurprising development given the hierarchy between teacher and student and their contrasting career ambitions.[19] This point is nevertheless important, to avoid an oversimplification of Martinican politics or intellectual life. Still, Césaire provided a vital role model for Fanon—a black intellectual who took advantage of the opportunities of French education and culture, but who was unafraid of confronting latent undercurrents of racism and political chauvinism.[20]

## Négritude

Négritude is essential for understanding the political culture of Martinique prior to and just after the Second World War. For Fanon, this black Francophone movement was his first formative intellectual influence. Often associated with the then-popular aesthetic of surrealism, Négritude had more complex origins than this common view can convey. As the literary scholar Brent Hayes Edwards has detailed, it drew upon multiple sources and venues across the Atlantic world, comprising a black internationalism, to use an expression by one of its vital predecessors, Jane Nardal (1902–1993).[21] Established in Paris during the 1930s by Césaire, Léopold Senghor (1906–2001), and Léon-Gontran Damas (1912–1978), it encompassed a range of literary figures. Senghor was from Senegal in French West Africa, which he would

47

later lead to independence, becoming its first president in 1960. Damas came from French Guiana in South America, though he also studied at the Lycée Schœlcher in Martinique, where he and Césaire first met as students. But equally important were the sisters Jane and Paulette Nardal (1896–1985) as well as Césaire's wife, Suzanne (1915–1966), all of whom were from Martinique and helped shape Négritude's meanings.[22]

Given its transatlantic geography, this intellectual movement must be understood as cosmopolitan in formation, but defined by perspectives from the margins of the French Empire. Like New York and London, Paris attracted writers, artists, and intellectuals from around the world, with gifted students from France's colonies attending its universities. But such cosmopolitanism was not circumscribed by imperial boundaries. Through the Nardal sisters, Césaire and his collaborators engaged the Harlem Renaissance and the efflorescence of African American cultural life during the same period, which marked the appearance of such figures as Langston Hughes (1902–1967), Zora Neale Hurston (1891–1960), and Claude McKay (1889–1948). The Black Atlantic and the alternative modernity it posed against European culture, as argued by sociologist Paul Gilroy, fully emerged during the first half of the twentieth century through the concurrent rise of Pan-Africanism, Garveyism, and Négritude.[23]

Like the former two movements, Négritude confronted the effects of racial discrimination and political inequality. But it adopted this mantle of political aspiration through cultural expression, primarily poetry. As the Nigerian literary critic Abiola Irele later commented, Négritude was at once a literary and ideological movement that signaled a "collective consciousness" that resisted the strictures of French colonialism.[24] It represented an act of counter-acculturation against the French policy of assimilation maintained during the nineteenth and early twentieth centuries, which promised equal citizenship and dignity provided that French language and moral values were adopted. Colonial subjects had to demonstrate their aptitude on French terms.[25] Négritude, in contrast, asserted a black identity that was not only positive—thus fighting against racist stereotypes of cultural primitivism and intellectual inferiority—but construed as civilizational, rather than merely local, in scope. Négritude argued for the innate unity of black culture, a common heritage that preceded Western colonialism. Yet, it implicitly worked within the French notion of "association" that stressed distinct cultures and pathways toward civilization.[26] Négritude therefore paralleled, but also retained specificity from, the Pan-Africanism espoused by Anglophone intellectuals like Henry Sylvester Williams (1869–1911) and W. E. B. Du Bois (1868–1963) during the same period, a movement which cited a shared experience of racism and political disenfranchisement across the Atlantic world from colonial Africa, to Europe, to the Americas.

It is important to stress, then, that Négritude as defined during the 1930s was not anticolonial. Though it condemned racial exclusion, it desired accommodation within French cultural life, not the end of French imperial rule as such—a key contrast with Fanon's vehement anticolonialism during the late 1950s and early 1960s. Reflecting on the expression in 1968, Damas remarked that Négritude "had a very precise meaning in the years 1934–35, namely the fact that the black man was seeking to know himself, that he wanted to become a historical actor and a cultural actor, and not just an object of domination or a consumer of culture. . . . The word 'negritude' was coined in the most racist moment of history, and we accepted the word *nègre* as a challenge."[27] Négritude thus presented an internal critical position both cultural and political in scope—a self-defined black humanism counterposed against a French colonial humanism that diminished African civilization.[28] Expressing its resistant stance in aesthetic fashion, Césaire demonstrated Négritude to powerful effect in his epic poem *Notebook of a Return to the Native Land* (*Cahier d'un retour au pays natal*, 1939), by conjuring in one section the spirit of Toussaint L'Ouverture and those who rebelled during the Haitian Revolution.[29]

The ambitions of Négritude therefore centered on sparring with the tacit limitations of long-standing colonial policies of assimilation, but without wholly rejecting French cultural and political ideals. Indeed, Césaire, Senghor, and Damas all wrote in French. They were all French citizens. Each eventually served in the French National Assembly at different points, representing their respective territories, and thus fulfilling what the policy of assimilation had promised—through the embrace of French civilization, a colonial subject could attain cultural citizenship and a measure of equality. Though Négritude did create a vital space for black culture, it retained a conservative quality, as Fanon would note, by primarily looking toward the past, not the future. Césaire and Senghor did turn toward a sharper rhetoric after the Second World War, as seen in Césaire's fierce polemic *Discourse on Colonialism* (1955) and Senghor's ascension to the presidency of Senegal.[30] But these shifts occurred in the wake of Négritude, which attained a peak in 1948 with the publication of an anthology of Négritude poetry edited by Senghor that included an influential preface by Sartre titled "Orphée noir" ("Black Orpheus"), Orpheus referring to the mythological Greek poet.

Sartre depicted Négritude as a form of antiracist racism—a race-based cultural movement intended to counter Eurocentrism. But, as such, it served as a temporary measure, part of a cultural dialectic that would lead to "the abolition of racial differences." "The unity which will come eventually, bringing all oppressed peoples together in the same struggle," Sartre argued, "must be preceded in the colonies by what I shall call the moment of separation or negativity," an instance of strategic essentialization that Négritude represented.[31] Though Sartre's preface introduced the work of Césaire, Senghor, and Damas to a wider audience, it also oversimplified Négritude's complex dimensions and foreclosed the possibility of an enduring black cultural autonomy, in a manner criticized as paternalistic.[32] Yet other black writers would sharply critique the movement. Echoing views articulated by Fanon in *Black Skin, White Masks*, the Nigerian playwright Wole Soyinka has cited Négritude not only as elitist, but as a project of romantic "race-retrieval" that problematically "adopted the Manichean tradition of European thought" and applied it to African societies that were "radically anti-Manichean." Négritude oversimplified African culture. It made no effort to understand the diversity of African cultural practices and values.[33]

Though Négritude began to decline before Fanon's intellectual maturation during the 1950s, it was an unavoidable influence on his early thinking, given its presence on Martinique. Césaire was not alone, but joined by his wife, Suzanne, and by René Ménil (1907–2004), who also taught at the Lycée Schœlcher. All three were involved in the journal *Tropiques* (founded in 1941), which promoted surrealism, critiques of colonialism, and anti-Vichy sentiments, given its establishment during World War II.[34] Yet Césaire in particular cast a shadow that Fanon both respected and sought to escape. Not only was Césaire a key figure within a pivotal group of black intellectuals, whose work André Breton (1896–1966), the founder of surrealism, praised highly, but their shared origins meant that engaging with Césaire in some fashion was unavoidable.[35] Césaire both liberated and constrained Fanon's ambitions. In an essay published in 1955, Fanon wrote, "Before Césaire, West Indian literature was a

literature of Europeans."[36] Césaire thus marked a fundamental shift. Fanon soon followed a path similar to his
former teacher's, but his intellectual future was still far
from certain on the eve of the Second World War. Indeed,
the conditions for Fanon's introduction to Europe proved
to be far more dramatic than attending school, leading
him down a different path from his esteemed predecessor.

# 2

# France

In the world I am heading for, I am endlessly creating myself.

I show solidarity with humanity provided I can go one step further.

—*Black Skin, White Masks*[1]

With the exception of Martinique, Frantz Fanon spent more years of his life in France than in any other country, including Algeria. The Second World War initiated this long, contentious relationship. The war significantly affected Martinique, as it did the rest of the French Empire. By the same stroke, it profoundly changed the course of Fanon's life. On June 22, 1940, the French government signed an armistice agreement with Nazi Germany, only eight days after German tanks had entered Paris and less than two months after Germany had invaded France. Its swift defeat astonished the international community and especially France's overseas colonies. This course of events generated an immediate response in support of resistance. Before the truce was signed, General Charles de Gaulle (1890–1970) rejected its terms and called on a Free French movement to liberate France from foreign occupation—a declaration known as the Appeal of June 18 (*L'Appel du 18 juin*), later broadcast by the BBC on June 22, 1940. He specifically called on France's imperial territories, declaring, "France is not alone. She has an immense Empire behind her."[2]

French colonies in Africa, Asia, and the Caribbean gradually aligned with de Gaulle, a bulk of support coming from Francophone Africa.[3] Popular political sentiment in Martinique also fell behind de Gaulle. Fanon's introduction to continental France consequently came through the roles of patriot and liberator. Movement forms an essential part of Fanon's personal history, constituting the extensive geography his life encompassed. His service in the Free French forces initiated this theme.

**Military Service**

Despite de Gaulle's appeal for imperial loyalty, the high commissioner for the French West Indies placed Martinique under the authority of the Vichy regime that collaborated with Nazi Germany. While the war in Europe may have been geographically distant, it did have a local impact, as it did in other parts of the empire. Shortages of food and other everyday needs became commonplace. Naval blockades contributed to this scarcity. Over time, this situation generated anxieties that cropped up in small acts of resistance—petty theft, sugarcane fields set ablaze—as well as desertion from the island. Fanon pursued this latter course of action, leaving Martinique in 1943, as did approximately 4,500 others during this period. He went north to the island of Dominica in order to join the Free French and received some basic military training. But he soon returned to Martinique, which fell under Free French control later that year. Fanon volunteered once more to fight overseas, and he left in 1944, against the wishes of his family, with the 5ème Bataillon de Marche des Antilles, a small infantry battalion.

After crossing the Atlantic via Bermuda, Fanon's unit was stationed in French-controlled Morocco for training, where it joined a diverse assemblage of military brigades that supported the Free French from across the empire.[4] Peter Geismar, in an early biography, writes that Fanon observed "noticeable barriers between the French from the metropolitan territory and the settlers in North Africa; both groups, though, looked down on the Moslems [sic] in the army, who [in turn] didn't care for the blacks. Fanon's company of soldiers, from Martinique, held aloof from the African troops, especially the Senegalese."[5] Such racial and cultural differences influenced Fanon's views regarding the diversity to be found across the French Empire and the pervasiveness of colonial racism—a fact that would later shape his political thinking. Fanon's time in North Africa also marked his introduction to Algeria. Stationed at Bougie (Béjaïa today) on the Algerian coast, Fanon was disturbed by the racism and poverty he encountered. "It was far worse than anything he had seen in the Caribbean," Geismar writes. "In Oran, Fanon had to watch French soldiers tossing crusts of bread to Moslem [*sic*] children fighting each other for the food. In Bougie, he went into a rage when he came upon Moslem children picking through military garbage."[6]

Fanon's unit ultimately formed part of Operation Dragoon, a plan promoted by de Gaulle to invade southern France from Algeria. In tandem with Operation Overlord—the D-Day assault on Normandy by American, British, Canadian, and Free French troops on June 6, 1944—this invasion would provide a counterassault from the south. The two operations combined would crush German forces occupying France. The Allied invasion of southern France began on August 15, though Fanon's battalion did not cross the Mediterranean until almost a month later on September 10. Fanon eventually joined a regiment of the *tirailleurs sénégalais*—as soldiers from Francophone West and Equatorial Africa were called— and later a European unit. As the season of autumn and their movement north progressed, Fanon endured challenging weather conditions in addition to combat. He suffered wounds from mortar fire in November 1944, eventually receiving the Croix de Guerre in February 1945 in recognition of his bravery. But any sense of honor this medal bestowed was paralleled by physical exhaustion, growing emotional discontent, and homesickness as the war reached its end in May 1945.

Indeed, the experience of fighting for France proved to be highly ambiguous for Fanon, with racism in its multiple forms generating a sense of constant unease. Despite a principle of shared patriotism, sharp differences materialized during his time in North Africa as indicated, with whites occupying the officer ranks and the tirailleurs sénégalais commanding the most respect among the colonial troops. Though Fanon and his two close friends from Martinique, Pierre Marie-Claire Mosole and Marcel Manville, were known as spirited troublemakers, Fanon remained deeply affected by his brief time in Algeria, due to the abject poverty and colonial racism there.[7] He himself faced discrimination from many Arab North Africans; they were not immune from racist French attitudes. In Europe, Fanon experienced further racism that many colonial troops were subjected to by local communities, despite their status as liberators. By the end of his service, he looked forward to returning to Martinique.

On his arrival home in October 1945, however, Fanon encountered Martinique with a different sense of the world. Though his military experience left him uncertain about his position as a French colonial, his decorated war service had provided him with an enlarged worldview—imperial in scope, but also beyond it. Alice Cherki writes that he was "disappointed to have taken part in the war, but his opposition to Nazism never wavered and the culture of the Resistance pervaded the whole of his life."[8] Fanon would later recall that the Second World War not only affected his perspective but changed how black Martinicans viewed France—a shift away from "the great white error" of an omniscient French colonialism that promised much, but offered little.[9]

Still, at the age of twenty, Fanon had an education to complete and a choice of career to make. The island of Martinique appeared small, with limited opportunity in the present and for the future. Contemplating both law and dentistry as options, Fanon passed his baccalaureate at the Lycée Schœlcher and left for France in 1946, with the benefit of state tuition support due to his veteran status. However, before leaving, Fanon, along with his brother Joby, worked for Césaire's campaign as the local communist party's candidate to represent Martinique in the French National Assembly.[10] Césaire already had been elected to the provisional postwar French assembly and as mayor of Fort-de-France in 1945, a position that he held for a remarkable fifty-six years until 2001. Césaire eventually served in the French National Assembly from 1946 to 1993. In fact, he supported Martinique's status as an overseas department—an often overlooked paradox given his political reputation and critical rhetoric later captured in *Discourse on Colonialism*.[11]

This political path would further distinguish Césaire from his former student.[12] Césaire would continue to believe in the possibilities of working within a revised framework of French republican ideals, whereas Fanon would gradually depart from this premise. Although Martinique continued to be home for Fanon for reasons of family, it started to recede into the backdrop from this moment of departure forward—being a place of origin, not destination.[13]

## An Elite Education

Joining his friends Manville and Mosole, Fanon arrived in Paris to study, but soon transferred to Lyon to pursue medicine—a part of France he was familiar with from his wartime service. It was an unlikely decision given the presence of his friends in Paris, as well as of his sister Gabrielle, who had recently moved to nearby Rouen. Similar to the war, this choice marked an initiation into French cultural life distinct from his Négritude predecessors. The provincial character of Lyon contrasted with Parisian cosmopolitanism. It was a time and place apart from the urbane life that Césaire and his compatriots embraced, a fact that Fanon would later reflect upon.[14]

His first year in Lyon was largely isolating. The sudden death of his father in 1947 enhanced feelings of loneliness and vulnerability. But compounding these sentiments was his ineluctable status as a racial minority, despite his privileged upbringing, his military service, and his French citizenship by birth. Fanon was well aware of this demographic limitation of Lyon, joking to his friend Manville, "there are too many Negroes in Paris, I want something more milky."[15] Among four hundred university students, fewer than twenty were black. Of those, most were from West Africa.[16]

But Lyon fortuitously reacquainted him with Algeria. A sizable Algerian community had been established there during the economic depression of the 1930s, forming part of the working class that labored in the city's factories.

Fanon's encounters with Algerian patients in Lyon would presage his future experiences during the Algerian War. In the meantime, he gradually developed a new social life. Though he did not become a formal member, Fanon was involved with the French Communist Party, in addition to the university's Overseas Students' Association—settings that stirred his political awakening. With education a priority, he took courses in chemistry, biology, and physics to make up for the limited qualifications in the sciences he had gained in Martinique, a necessity before he could formally undertake medical school. This narrow background not only left him unprepared for certain aspects of medicine but also reinforced his literary bent: Fanon was soon drawn to lectures and readings in philosophy, phenomenology, and psychoanalysis.[17]

It is important to stress the differences between psychiatry—a medical field that treats mental health as part of the biological functioning of the brain and human nervous system—and psychoanalysis—a field pioneered by Sigmund Freud (1856–1939), who was trained as a neurologist, but stressed the importance of lived experience, rather than intrinsic biological nature, in determining psychological fitness. David Macey has argued that this distinction is often overlooked by readers of Fanon, who tend to view his pioneering perspectives strictly on psychoanalytic grounds.[18] The conflation of these fields can partly be attributed to the prominence and influence of psychoanalysts, such as Jacques Lacan (1901–1981), in France during the 1950s. While it is true that Fanon specifically trained as a psychiatrist, it is fair to argue that psychoanalysis had a significant bearing on his thinking, given its general influence at the time and its particular validation for treating patients on an individual basis, rather than institutionally through asylums and hospitals—a phenomenon that had spanned Europe during the nineteenth century, resulting in the confinement of many. Fanon's entry into the field therefore occurred at an exciting time when the discipline of psychiatry was undergoing a stimulating redefinition, motivated by the popularity of psychoanalysis. Both trends held appeal for the self-searching student.

Other developments were also afoot. Fanon arrived during a vital period in French intellectual life, when a number of thinkers were grappling with the effects and meaning of the Second World War. His enrollment in classes given in the philosophy department at Lyon, where he attended lectures by the phenomenologist Maurice Merleau-Ponty (1908–1961), is indicative of his engagement with this emergent scene.[19] The war occasioned many disasters and challenges of broad human importance—the rise of fascism and totalitarianism, the Holocaust and its genocidal violence, and the advent of the nuclear age, among them—that raised fundamental questions of individual ethics and community politics for the postwar period. Like Fanon, some—such as Jean-Paul Sartre and Albert Camus (1913–1960)—had directly participated in the war, as members of the Free French. Other intellectuals—Simone de Beauvoir (1908–1986) and the

African American writer Richard Wright (1908–1960), then based in Paris—applied similar scrutiny to intensifying issues of gender and race in the public sphere.

This intellectual milieu represented in part by the journal *Les Temps modernes,* edited by Sartre and de Beauvoir, paralleled and interacted with the intellectual circle surrounding *Présence africaine,* the leading journal of black culture published in France. Founded in 1947 by Alioune Diop (1910–1980), a Senegalese writer, *Présence africaine* provided a crucial literary venue for the Négritude movement, but it embraced pan-African concerns more generally. Comparing *Présence africaine* to *Les Temps modernes,* the philosopher V. Y. Mudimbe has written that the former sought "to bring in the very center of . . . French power and culture what was being negated in [the] colonies, that is, the dignity of otherness."[20] *Présence africaine,* put simply, sought "to incarnate the voice of a silenced Africa."[21] These two publications consequently framed the intellectual world within which Fanon intended to find a place.

Unlike Négritude, Fanon first encountered French continental philosophy primarily through reading, not personal connections. The prevalent trends were phenomenology and existentialism. Interrelated in scope, these philosophical approaches built on the nineteenth-century thought of German philosopher Georg W. F. Hegel (1770–1831), who argued that individual consciousness emerged dialectically between a person and the world, rather than solely through individual deductive reasoning as proposed by René Descartes (1596–1650), the French thinker considered to be the founder of modern philosophy. Drawing on Immanuel Kant (1724–1804) and his *Critique of Pure Reason* (1781), Hegel's engaged method has since become known as phenomenology, as captured in his work *The Phenomenology of the Spirit* (1807). Among its most influential sections is the rumination on lordship and bondage—more often referred to as the master-slave dialectic—that articulated how self-consciousness (and power) depended on the presence of another person.[22] Martin Heidegger (1889–1976), drawing on the parallel work of Søren Kierkegaard (1813–1855) and his own mentor Edmund Husserl (1859–1938), extended phenomenology's parameters in *Being and Time* (1927), to consider factors of place and time for further defining the dimensions of self-consciousness. One's existence was not solely shaped by the presence of others, but also by these two situated aspects.

These sources of thought from the nineteenth and early twentieth centuries that largely originated from a German philosophical tradition fundamentally informed the French phenomenology and existentialism that Fanon encountered. *Being and Nothingness* (1943) by Sartre and *Phenomenology of Perception* (1945) by Merleau-Ponty outlined French variations of these philosophical approaches, stressing the importance of personal experience and perception for self-realization. These ideas soon reached a popular audience, with Sartre's *Anti-Semite and Jew* (1946) and de Beauvoir's *The Second*

*Sex* (1949) powerfully utilizing the roles of public perception and regard for understanding the construction of specific social group identities, rather than dwelling on the individual alone.

This burst of philosophical inquiry held considerable appeal for a European intelligentsia recovering from the devastating effects of a war that had destroyed much of the continent physically, culturally, and morally. The notion of an indifferent world as conveyed by existentialism resonated with a public coping with the aftermath of violence and genocide—a sentiment reinforced by the absurdism and nihilism in popular fiction like Camus's *The Stranger* (1942), set in his native Algeria.[23] Existentialism's argument for free will, which drew on Friedrich Nietzsche (1844–1900) as well as Kierkegaard, and the concurrent need to recognize and work against "bad faith"—a practice of self-deception defined by aspirations to meet generic social standards or political demands, but ultimately preventing individual fulfillment—provided one answer for creating meaning in an uncertain postwar era.[24]

This prescription for self-actualization caught the attention of Fanon, as it did for so many—as did the bridging of academic and public realms. Indeed, Fanon's interest in phenomenology and existentialism is readily understandable, given his early engagement with Négritude and surrealism through Aimé Césaire. Like psychiatry and these aesthetic movements, the philosophical approaches of phenomenology and existentialism drew on notions of the conscious and the unconscious and the vital importance in understanding these realms to advance and consummate self-understanding. Fanon's early attempts at writing included plays in the vein of Sartre's existential dramas. But these philosophical influences had a greater bearing on the manuscript that would result in *Black Skin, White Masks,* which soon preoccupied him—as did rapid developments in his personal and professional life.

Fanon became romantically involved with two women during this period—experiences that likely informed his essays on gender and interracial relationships in his first book. Fanon had one child, Mireille, out of wedlock with a fellow medical student in 1948. His eventual neglect of this relationship can be attributed to the relationship he soon had with his future wife, Marie-Josephe Dublé (1931–1989), better known as Josie Fanon, whom he met in 1949.[25] Dublé came from a politically progressive background; her parents were trade unionists. Fanon and Dublé married in 1952. These personal changes overlapped with several equally fast professional transitions.

His first assignment after his formal medical coursework was a temporary internship at the Saint-Ylié psychiatric hospital in Dôle, north of Lyon, where he encountered a woman whose illness involved anxiety toward black people: a case included in his first book. In fact, Fanon had originally planned to submit a thesis focusing on psychiatric issues of race—an early version of *Black Skin, White Masks*—which was thwarted by his advisor, Jean Dechaume (1896–1968), resulting in a more conventional dissertation on Friedreich's ataxia—a hereditary disease that causes the nervous system to degenerate—submitted, after his time in Dôle, in 1951.[26] Nevertheless, Fanon referenced Lacan and stressed a diagnostic method that identified social relations and "the lived history of the subject" as determining factors for psychological health, in contrast to strictly physiological explanations.[27] A new position at the Saint-Alban psychiatric hospital in the Loire Valley provided an opportunity to develop his budding psychiatric approach.

Under the guidance of François Tosquelles (1912–1994)—a Spanish psychiatrist, anti-fascist against the Franco regime, and founder of an institutional psychotherapy movement that would become influential—Saint-Alban was an experimental facility that encouraged interaction between patients, doctors, and staff such that traditional doctor-patient hierarchies were broken down and a sense of communal healing emerged. Anticipating arguments popularized by historian-philosopher Michel Foucault (1926–1984) regarding the asylum as a site of power, this innovative form of sociotherapy diminished feelings of difference, alienation, and exclusion among patients—a perspective on treatment and respect that strongly influenced Fanon's later work ethic in Algeria.[28] "The aim was not to muzzle madness but to question and listen to it in order to create the conditions for new structures [for rehabilitation]," writes Cherki. "The method at Saint-Alban, very new at the time, was premised on a communal arrangement in which [the] sane and the insane lived together as caregivers and boarders inside an institutional framework."[29]

This early professional experience lasting fifteen months thus shaped Fanon's medical approach in profound ways, particularly in terms of direct engagement with, and empathy for, patients.[30] Fanon, moreover, deeply admired Tosquelles for his antifascist politics.[31] After a brief return in 1952 to Martinique that proved disappointing in terms of finding work—as fate would have it, his last visit there—Fanon returned to Lyon and eventually passed his licensing exams in June 1953 with the help of Tosquelles. He then took an ill-suited interim position as the head physician at a hospital in Pontorson in northwest France, near Mont Saint-Michel. He sought to apply the techniques he learned at Saint-Alban—"to shake up the system, to give the patients a voice"—but found resistance. Still, as Cherki recalls, "He bent many an ear to this end, and his reputation as a revolutionary in the field, which persists to this day, was established in the process."[32]

Fanon was also gradually establishing himself as a groundbreaking thinker in another field. Several months before he passed his exams in 1953, his first book, *Black Skin, White Masks,* appeared. He had previously published two articles in *Esprit,* a leftist monthly journal similar in scope to the better-known *Les Temps modernes.* These essays published in May 1951 and February 1952 concerned, respectively, "the lived experience of the black man"—a piece to be later included in *Black Skin, White Masks*—and the so-called North African syndrome, a psychosomatic condition Fanon encountered among Lyon's Algerian immigrants, who suffered from physical ailments that he attributed to social alienation. Though *Esprit* published such distinguished contributors as philosopher Paul Ricœur (1913–2005) and antitorture critic Pierre Vidal-Naquet (1930–2006), David Macey has noted that the appearance of these essays in *Esprit* was unusual.[33] A more obvious venue would have been *Présence africaine*. Still, *Esprit* took a critical view toward French colonialism, had Algerian and other North African writers as contributors, and published pieces on psychiatry—a combination that resonated with Fanon.

Éditions du Seuil published *Esprit,* and it subsequently became Fanon's publisher for *Black Skin, White Masks.* Unlike his supervisor in Lyon, his editor at Seuil, Francis Jeanson (1922–2009), understood the social and political importance of Fanon's writing with its focus on race and its dehumanizing effects across racial lines.[34] In his preface to the book, Jeanson wrote, "Fanon is speaking for these people, for all his real brothers and all his living sisters—just as he is speaking for all those [whites] who, because they fail to recognize them and challenge their membership of [*sic*] the human race, therefore fail to recognize themselves and exclude themselves from the human race."[35]

Though Fanon had the strong backing of his editor, *Black Skin, White Masks* failed to draw wide attention initially: a consequence of Fanon's status as a first-time author; the relative marginality of black writing in France;

and the unusual nature of the book itself with its constituent elements of race, psychology, and philosophy, which left uncertain its intended audience. The book exacerbated this problem at a basic level. Full of insights, it nevertheless was difficult to read, with its combination of technical terms, unusual source material, and individual meditation. As a whole, it defied easy categorization. While general connections can be drawn between its themes of black identity and the subconscious and those explored by the Négritude movement, these broad affinities are not consistently meaningful. Fanon sought a different approach. The assemblage of references in *Black Skin, White Masks* clearly positioned it as an academic study, not poetic literature as such. And yet it was undeniably personal, searching for a language of expression beyond mere conveyance of information and argument. The essays that make up *Black Skin, White Masks* foreground the nature of individual experience. They reflected Fanon's life up to that point—and a growing sense of estrangement.

Categorizing Fanon as mentioned before is a risky practice. It is also unnecessary. His originality derives from his mutual interests across the disciplines of psychiatry, psychoanalysis, and philosophy—a complex, yet interrelated, set of concerns that gained their first expression in *Black Skin, White Masks.* He was only twenty-seven. Though Fanon would later speak little of his first book, it provided a basis for his thinking and writing that would continue to evolve and mature in the years ahead.[36]

**3**

# *Black Skin, White Masks*

For the black man there is only one destiny.
And it is white.
                                    —*Black Skin, White Masks*[1]

*Black Skin, White Masks* marks the beginning of Frantz
Fanon's life as a public intellectual. It is arguably his most
influential book, more so than *The Wretched of the Earth*,
given its attention to enduring, universal issues of race
and identity. Indeed, its popular reemergence during the
1980s as a canonical text can be attributed to these themes,
which his last book does not address as fully.[2] But *Black
Skin, White Masks* is equally important for the individual
meaning it had for Fanon. It presented a summation of
his formal education. By the same stroke, it documented
the start of his break from France and Martinique alike.
As his most psychiatric book by far, Fanon inhabits *Black
Skin, White Masks* as both doctor and patient—diagnosing
the conscious and unconscious ailments of racism, while
also inserting himself as a victim of such conditions. The
book similarly builds on two intellectual trends in France
that characterized the postwar period—phenomenology

and existentialism—with their two main proponents—Maurice Merleau-Ponty and Jean-Paul Sartre, respectively—influencing Fanon in profound ways. They offered methods for thinking through the connections between individual perception, lived experience, and the creation of social identity. Fanon sought to enter this intellectual conversation. For him, being black was the result of being perceived as black, rather than resting within an innate essence—a contrast with Négritude.

It is equally important to place Fanon and his first book within the political context of postwar France. The constitution of the Fourth Republic (1946–58), which Aimé Césaire and Léopold Senghor helped to write, granted citizenship across the French Empire. But rather than assuaging political voices in the colonies, this bold move only revitalized debate over the meanings of assimilation, association, and citizenship amid broader questions regarding the future. The indispensable support of France's colonies during the war along with political moments like the Brazzaville Conference (1944), which had promised reform, generated widespread tensions between restructuring an imperial status quo versus colonies seeking complete independence. French Indochina quickly undertook armed struggle, while other colonies considered alternatives such as federation within a greater France.[3]

Fanon engaged with such sweeping issues only indirectly, though his arguments were still embedded in this context of uncertainty. *Black Skin, White Masks* grapples with the meaning of being both black and French. It is critical of assimilation, yet not anticolonial in a conventional sense. It articulates a more radical stance as compared to Négritude, even obliquely calling for social revolution, but not decolonization per se, as in his later work. It is primarily concerned with the individual rather than the community, unlike *The Wretched of the Earth*. This chapter consequently summons a more complex reading of this text that resists a common approach which has unvaryingly labeled it as anticolonial. Political thought in imperial contexts, even among the colonized, is not often so easily reducible. Destiny presents a constant problem when understanding Fanon in particular, as cited earlier. Nevertheless, Fanon firmly underscored the pervasiveness of colonial racism and, ultimately, the limited significance of French citizenship—the fact of blackness in the face of French nonracial claims to the contrary.[4]

## Situating *Black Skin, White Masks*

Other black intellectuals had previously addressed the correlation between visibility and racism. W. E. B. Du Bois's idea of double consciousness—the proposition that African American identity was defined through the attitudes of white Americans, in addition to African American self-perception—in *The Souls of Black Folk* (1903) captured earlier the implications of seeing and being seen for notions of racial subjectivity and discrimination. The novel *Invisible Man* (1952) by Ralph Ellison (1914–1994), coincidentally published the same year as *Black Skin,*

*White Masks,* similarly foregrounded such themes, as the title itself highlights, in order to depict the plight of African Americans in a society that refused to acknowledge their presence.[5]

Yet *Black Skin, White Masks* retains an unparalleled originality. As with these other works, it is a powerful critique of white racism. It is a searching evaluation of black psychology as well. Fanon's title insinuates this diagnostic appraisal at the outset, positing a tension between blackness as being defined by unconscious aspirations to be white versus the existence of an autonomous black identity beyond such problematic assimilationist ambitions, behind such masks. His growing estrangement from Martinique and France, partly a result of his war service, fostered this critical position toward black behavior and white racism alike. In referencing African American writers such as Richard Wright and Chester Himes (1909–1984), both of whom spent considerable time in France, Fanon lamented the constraints of his own French citizenship as similar to the predicament of African Americans, who also had equal citizenship in name, but not in practice.

However, *Black Skin, White Masks* is a work decidedly within a mid-twentieth-century French intellectual tradition. It is deeply informed by academic trends and political debates at the time. Consisting of seven interrelated essays plus an introduction and conclusion, it spans a diverse set of subjects including language, sexuality, colonialism, the politics of social recognition, and questions of psychopathology. This thematic range reflected Fanon's personal interests and professional training, as well as his holistic approach to the problem of racism. "It is one of the original and disturbing qualities of *Black Skin, White Masks* that it rarely historicizes the colonial experience," writes Homi K. Bhabha. "There is no master narrative or realist perspective that provides a background of social and historical facts against which emerge the problems of the individual or collective psyche."[6] While it is true that Fanon does not delve into historical detail, the idiosyncratic assortment of topics found in his first book is predicated on an argument for the connections between these varied empirical experiences and self-knowledge. They cannot be comprehended either in isolation or through pure abstraction. For example, understandings of race and sexuality—the latter a perennially popular topic among psychoanalysts—defined one another through culturally circulated ideas of group preference and difference. Both, in turn, could contribute to forms of individual psychological distress. The colony was one context in which these symptoms manifested.

This layered eclecticism reflects Fanon's attempts at depicting a type of *psychological realism*—a grounded dialectic between the social and the unconscious. It also explains the book's relative obscurity upon publication. Fanon's text was neither a scientific study nor a philosophical treatise. Tonally, he ranges from the sobriety of clinical diagnoses, to crass humor when speaking of sex, to bitter sarcasm and anger when addressing the vicissitudes of French racism, to unguarded sincerity when declaring his own shortcomings. Yet, despite its intensely personal features—Fanon was, after all, an exemplary *assimilé* (one who had assimilated)—it was not a memoir. In many ways, *Black Skin, White Masks* is best read piecemeal, rather than with the assumption that it possesses an overarching narrative structure. Meditative in character, it is not programmatic like *The Wretched of the Earth,* outlining revolutionary strategy at a societal level. Nor does it contain the descriptive immediacy of the political reportage found in *A Dying Colonialism* and *Toward the African Revolution.* It is, above all, an interrogatory work: its ambitions rest in the author's desire to raise fundamental questions about race through the prisms of his occupational and life experiences.

Still, *Black Skin, White Masks* prefigures these later books—not because it appeared first, but because it laid out a set of problems that Fanon grappled with for the rest of his life. These inquiries can be summarized progressively as follows: how to live as a black man, how to live as a colonized person, and how to transcend these mutually reinforced conditions that constrained free will and, ultimately, humanity. Indeed, it must be emphasized once more that Fanon was a French citizen, not a colonial subject as such. Like his African American peers, Fanon interrogated the limits of modern citizenship attributable to race. Like Césaire and Senghor, he was also thinking within a particular postwar milieu defined by the Fourth Republic and its escalating internal debates—imperial in scope—over competing possibilities and meanings of citizenship, cultural assimilation, and political independence. The Second World War generated far-reaching pressures from Europe's overseas colonies, which demanded rights and reform in the wake of their wartime support.

For Fanon, this political premise led to consideration of the nature of a specific black "ontology"—its emergence, its contours, its uses, and its meanings. As with Négritude, this deeper inquiry into black being or existence was essential, given its implications for political belonging. What could French citizenship mean, if racism not only diminished its promised entitlements, but denied the basic humanity of those defined as citizens? Fanon concluded that a specific black ontology did exist, but that its viability was rendered inferior due to its formation through white racist perceptions. In fact, Fanon contended that this ontology resulted not just from a situation of external dehumanization by whites but, more provocatively, from a situation of uncritical black self-oppression through assimilationist tendencies. In principle then, one of his intended readerships was a black petit bourgeoisie. As indicated with his opening epigraph from Césaire's *Discourse on Colonialism,* Fanon sought to contribute to an existing intellectual tradition that addressed the "millions of men who have been skillfully injected with fear, inferiority complexes, trepidation, servility, despair, [and] abasement."[7]

Fanon nonetheless questioned his reasons for writing this book—a manifestation of its status as a first book and, by extension, a first-time author's concerns for audience and reception. It must be emphasized that he was only twenty-seven when it appeared in print. The introduction is bold in its stated goal of "the liberation of the man of color from himself," thus serving as a step toward "a new humanism"—a phrase that resembles Césaire's idea of a "true humanism" and that Steve Biko (1946–1977), a founder of South Africa's Black Consciousness Movement, would later embrace and reformulate to envision a future South Africa.[8] Nevertheless, Fanon inserts caveats and self-doubt, indicating the magnitude of the issues at hand and his individual self-awareness. "I do not come with timeless truths," he writes at the outset. "My consciousness is not illuminated with ultimate radiances."[9]

This introductory contrast of ambition and reservation prefigures tensions throughout the book between the individual and society, the subjective and the universal, medical diagnoses and humanistic interpretation, and, not least, between being a clinical study versus a personal statement for social change. Fanon stressed his subjective view ("Since I was born in the Antilles, my observations and my conclusions are valid only for the Antilles") and how his ideas were fixed to a particular time ("The architecture of this work is rooted in the temporal. Every human problem must be considered from the standpoint of time. Ideally, the present will always contribute to the building of the future").[10] Indeed, Fanon dictated *Black Skin, White Masks* to his wife, Josie—a fact that illuminates its unique voice and prose style of aphoristic insights and reflective asides. He drew on his own thoughts, feelings, and first-hand experiences from the immediacy of memory and the cathartic act of speaking aloud, without automatically resorting to an academic literature to contextualize or justify his ideas. In this boldly psychiatric fashion—a version of the so-called talking cure—Fanon did not literally write his first book so much as verbally articulate it. Rather than limiting the reach and meaning of his ideas, these qualities of spontaneity and specificity ultimately explain the book's resilience.[11]

## Negotiating Blackness and Whiteness

To begin a walk-through of the text, Fanon lays out in the introduction a diverse set of statements, problems, and questions that, overall, seek a prognosis for the "massive psycho-existential complex" resulting from "the juxtaposition of the black and white races."[12] Only by "analyzing it" is it possible to "destroy it."[13] Fanon focuses explicit concern on the emergence of a black inferiority complex and how it had both broad socioeconomic dimensions and personal psychological elements.[14] He uses the term *sociogeny*—referring to the social development of the individual—to capture the relationship between these two realms.[15] His consequent approach is decidedly multifaceted. "I shall be derelict. I leave methods to the botanists and the mathematicians," he notes in cavalier fashion. "There is a point at which methods devour themselves."[16] Self-deprecation aside, this polyvalent quality must be understood as a mode of experimentation, a search for an original diagnostic appraisal, and the sub-sequent positioning of a new critical vocabulary. In this regard, Fanon's primary contribution is his depiction of the Manichean (or dualistic) structure of the colonial situation along racial lines, a model that remains widely influential today. But, contrary to popular belief, Fanon did not seek to reinforce this structure. Rather, given its colonial origins, he endeavored to move beyond it, by demonstrating its interactive character and, therefore, the possibilities of transcending it.

Chapter 1 launches this critical assessment. Titled "The Black Man and Language," it confronts the limits of cultural assimilation through the acquisition of French language skills—specifically, how black citizens and colonial subjects, despite the attainment of such ability, were not treated as equal due to their race. Echoing Du Bois's argument for double consciousness, Fanon begins by writing that the "black man possesses two dimensions: one with his fellow Blacks, the other with the Whites. A black man behaves differently with a white man than he does with another black man. There is no doubt whatsoever that this fissiparousness is a direct consequence of the colonial undertaking."[17] The cultural setting of colonialism is what distinguishes Fanon from Du Bois. Indeed, Fanon underscores an imperial geography for this predicament of doubleness, and the additional differences between educated colonial subjects who move to imperial metropolises, like Paris, and those subjects who remain in the colonies. The inferiority complex of the former is intensified through a type of geographic assimilation that results in a separation from home and a concluding sense of alienation.

Exacerbating this displacement are language and the treatment of *évolués*—literally, those who "evolved"—by the French. "To speak a language is to appropriate its world and culture," Fanon observes. "The Antillean who wants to be white will succeed, since he will have adopted the cultural tool of language."[18] Yet this adoption does not guarantee equality. "The fact is that the European has a set idea of the black man," Fanon maintains, "and there is nothing more exasperating than to hear: 'How long have you lived in France? You speak such good French.'"[19] He consequently positions language acquisition as emblematic of the contradictions of assimilation. The achievement of French language skills—and French, it must be stressed, was Fanon's native tongue, in addition to Antillean Creole—is a key measure of this process, universally attainable through study. But, in practice, complete assimilation and equal citizenship are not possible. A "retaining-wall relation between language and group" prevents their full realization.[20] This opening essay therefore signals an additional meaning of the book's title, with white masks indicating white duplicity and the concealment of true intentions—even the ultimate unknowability of whiteness.

This introductory discussion sets up the more complicated matter of interracial relationships as a path for social assimilation and the roles of gender and sexuality in shaping racial identities. Here too, personal experience—what Ato Sekyi-Otu has called "immediate knowledge"—informs Fanon's argumentation, if implicitly.[21] Fanon frames these relationships within a duality of aggression versus love, drawing from Sartre and his notion of being-for-others: social relationships are defined by power, with one's identity and status subject to the recognition and regard of other people. Racial difference can present an obstacle to achieving "authentic love" between a black person and a white person, due to socially conditioned feelings of inferiority and superiority.[22] As critic David Marriott writes, the possibility of attaining this love, in Fanon's view, recedes when "sex and desire are constrained by [such racial] myths."[23]

Addressing how black Martinican women aspired to be with white men, Fanon critiques their assimilationist desire for "lactification," a whitening of black identity.[24] Any "Antillean woman in her flirtations and her liaisons will prefer the lighter-skinned man," he observes. "We know a lot of girls from Martinique, students in France, who confess in lily-white innocence that they would never marry a black man."[25] Chapter 3, titled "The Man of Color and the White Woman," continues this argument. "I wish to be acknowledged not as *black* but as *white*," Fanon states, characterizing the views of a number of black men. "Now—and this is a form of recognition that Hegel had not envisaged—who but a white woman can do this for me? By loving me she proves that I am worthy of white love. I am loved like a white man. I am a white man."[26] Yet, as with language, these modes of assimilation through sexual intimacy are problematic for the self-esteem and psychic health of black women and men.[27] Aspiring to be white diminishes senses of self, as he knew firsthand.

These first three chapters that focus primarily on the individual—and principally originate from European philosophy—are followed by an engagement with psychoanalysis as an alternative method for understanding race and colonialism. This technique's emphasis on the psyche raised a new set of concerns for Fanon: though racism and alienation may not be entirely individual, neither could they be construed as wholly uniform. Fanon's reservations about a strictly psychoanalytic approach are found in chapter 4's sharp critique of Octave Mannoni (1899–1989) and his book *Prospero and Caliban: The Psychology of Colonization* (1950), a work Fanon considered "dangerous."[28] The title refers to two characters in William Shakespeare's *The Tempest* (1610–11), Prospero being exiled with his daughter, Miranda, to an island occupied by Caliban, whom Prospero eventually enslaves. This setting and relationship of power provided Mannoni with an allegory to capture the nature of French colonialism in Madagascar. Mannoni had served as an administrator there, which had been a French colony since 1895. He witnessed the Malagasy Uprising (1947–48), involving 15,000 to 20,000 rebels and resulting in a death toll estimated to range from 11,000 to 100,000 Malagasies. Mannoni subsequently argued that the colonial situation could be understood on psychological grounds, approximating a relationship between parent and child, with colonized Malagasies suffering from an inferiority complex that further incurred a dependency complex.

Fanon criticizes this interpretation that suggested an innate psychological predisposition for colonial rule. He commends Mannoni for recognizing that "the problem of colonialism" included the role of "human attitudes."[29] But Mannoni's suggestion that the inferiority complex among colonized peoples was intrinsic and permanent is wrong. Fanon agrees that "the confrontation of 'civilized' and 'primitive' men" brought about "the *emergence* of a mass of illusions and misunderstandings that only a psychological analysis can place and define."[30] And yet, Fanon asks, "Why does he [Mannoni] try to make the inferiority complex something that antedates colonization?"[31] "The feeling of inferiority of the colonized is the correlative to the European's feeling of superiority," he asserts. "Let us have the courage to say it outright: *It is the racist who creates his inferior.*"[32] Fanon's ensuing secondary criticism is that Mannoni "leaves the Malagasy no choice save between inferiority and dependence. . . . There is no salvation."[33] Fanon contends, in contrast, that the consequences of colonialism "were not psychological alone" and that the colonial subject is "in a position to *choose* action (or passivity) with respect to the real source of the conflict—that is, toward the social structures."[34] "As a psychoanalyst, I should help my patient to become *conscious* of his unconscious and abandon his attempts at a hallucinatory whitening," Fanon remarks.[35]

If "the 'dependency complex' of the Malagasy" exists, it "originates with the arrival on the island of the white colonizers."[36]

Overall, in this chapter and the preceding ones, Fanon outlines scenarios and critical methods for understanding colonial racism and its psychological effects. He identifies the Manichean character of French rule in diverse settings to underscore its political ubiquity, assess its ideological strengths, and highlight its local weaknesses. Indeed, a broader agenda materializes in these chapters, which steps beyond his warnings of individual self-destructive behavior. An institutionalized problem of racism existed, with a concurrent need for political engagement at a systemic level—a position Fanon would articulate further in the years ahead.

## Nights of the Absolute

These first chapters distinguish Fanon as a contrarian. Moving beyond subjective observation alone, he presented philosophical and psychological interpretations of racial experience to counter accepted stereotypes and cultural practices. He foregrounded sociopolitical arguments when problematic psychoanalytic explanations, as with Mannoni, were offered. He similarly utilized then-innovative clinical terminology from psychiatry when dissatisfied with the analytic rigor of humanistic appraisals. Diagnoses such as the "abandonment-neurotic"—a personality type based on the experience of abandonment in early childhood, in turn generating

85

a psychological condition characterized by low self-esteem and insecurity—and the "negative-aggressive"—a personality type who turns such feelings of devaluation into forms of aggression—endeavored to move beyond conventional cultural observation, offering deeper analysis beyond acknowledged social hierarchies of race. This shifting methodology does not reflect ambivalence or the absence of an agenda. Rather, this versatility presented a critique of existing methods and highlights Fanon's ambition to think beyond the conventions of disciplinary reason, to test the possibilities of alternative paradigms for a more holistic understanding of race and racism.[37] *Black Skin, White Masks* intended to plot a new approach between philosophy and psychology that resisted the omniscience of either.

These initial chapters that maneuver between these fields set the stage for chapter 5, which forms the crux of Fanon's book. Originally titled "The Fact of Blackness" in the 1967 English translation, chapter 5 was retitled in the 2008 version as "The Lived Experience of the Black Man"—a difference that emphasizes racial identity as a social formation rather than a pre-given, permanent condition.[38] This chapter struggles with being black and French at once. It remains one of Fanon's best-known essays. "'Dirty nigger!' or simply 'Look! A Negro!'" the chapter provocatively begins, underscoring the relational aspect of racial identification.[39] The meaning of this startling episode—a moment of public recognition in the vein of Sartre—goes deeper than the shouting of a racist epithet. It underlines how black existence is fundamentally circumscribed by white racism—a profound limitation on having any sense of free will. "As long as the black man remains on his home territory, except for petty internal quarrels, he will not have to experience his being for others," Fanon writes. But, for many, this autonomy was unattainable, since "any ontology" was rendered "impossible in a colonized and acculturated society."[40] Even the notion of ontology—a common philosophical term referring to being or existence—presented explanatory problems for Fanon. "Ontology does not allow us to understand the being of the black man, since it ignores the lived experience," he continues. "For not only must the black man be black; he must be black in relation to the white man."[41] Against this situation, Fanon contends that only positive self-assertion can resist the problems of white recognition. "I made up my mind, since it was impossible to rid myself of an *innate complex,* to assert myself as a BLACK MAN," he declares. "Since the Other was reluctant to recognize me, there was only one answer: to make myself known."[42]

But such actions could be difficult to undertake and maintain. As a black man, Fanon felt "overdetermined from the outside" based on his skin color.[43] "I am a slave not to the 'idea' others have of me," Fanon deduces, "but to my appearance."[44] This epidermal condition first signaled in the book's title generated a kind of nausea, due to varying public judgments of recognition, acceptance, scorn, and rejection.[45] Nausea is an existential concept introduced in Sartre's first novel of the same name, a work that explored the existential angst later articulated in *Being and Nothingness*. "Shame. Shame and self-contempt. Nausea," Fanon remarks in sequence. "When they like me, they tell me my color has nothing to do with it. When they hate me, they add that it's not because of my color. Either way, I am a prisoner of the vicious circle."[46]

Fanon ultimately attributes this nausea that captured physical and philosophical meanings to the contradiction between French claims to nonracialism through cultural assimilation and legal citizenship, yet the continued reinforcement of racial difference. The fact of racism stood against the professed promise of European Enlightenment ideals, which promoted scientific reason against unfounded superstition and belief—a point that philosopher Lewis Gordon has expanded on in relation to Fanon. In Gordon's words, it is through the critical thought of Fanon that "we learn that the twentieth-century person of color embodies a crisis of Europe and Euro-reason."[47] "I had rationalized the world, and the world had rejected me in the name of color prejudice," Fanon himself observes. "Since there was no way we could agree on the basis of reason, I resorted to irrationality. It was up to the white man to be more irrational than I."[48]

This turn toward the irrational—in Fanon's sardonic manner—refers to Négritude. Yet this cultural movement presented limitations as well, due to its acceptance of French notions of racial difference. *Black Skin, White Masks* remains an important early critique of Négritude.

In "Black Orpheus," the preface to Léopold Senghor's 1948 anthology, Sartre argues that Négritude is a form of anti-racist racism and as such a necessary dialectical stage toward a society without racism.[49] Critical of this mechanical view, Fanon expresses that he felt "robbed" of his "last chance."[50] Sartre misunderstood the purpose of Négritude, which holds that "consciousness needs to get lost in the night of the absolute, the only condition for attaining self-consciousness."[51] "*Black Orpheus* marks a date in the intellectualization of black *existence*," Fanon submits. "And Sartre's mistake was not only to seek the source of the spring, but in a certain way to drain the spring dry."[52] Fanon subsequently argues that such analysis, even in support, could be disabling—"Jean-Paul Sartre has destroyed black impulsiveness"—rather than liberating.[53] "I need to lose myself totally in negritude [*sic*]," Fanon professes.[54] "Without a black past, without a black future, it was impossible for me to live my blackness," he laments. "Not yet white, no longer completely black, I was damned."[55] Yet Négritude also suffers critique. Fanon refers to it as "this wretched romanticism" and emphasizes that "the black experience is ambiguous, for there is not *one* Negro—there are *many* black men."[56] Négritude may provide a means to attain self-consciousness, but it does not explain the diversity of racism. Being black does not depend on a civilizational essence. It is based on lived experience.

Finding no solution through either French political ideals or Négritude, Fanon returns once more to psychiatry and psychoanalysis in chapter 6, the longest and the most technical discussion in *Black Skin, White Masks.* His approach is less personal, and it can be assumed that this chapter formed part of his planned thesis submission. Bringing together themes from the preceding chapters, Fanon is concerned again with the relationship between "psychopathology"—mental distress and illness—and race. One result is that the "black man stops behaving as an *actional* person."[57] "His actions are destined for 'the Other' (in the guise of the white man)," Fanon writes, "since only 'the Other' can enhance his status and give him self-esteem at the ethical level."[58] Fanon also revisits the issue of sexuality. "As regards the black man everything in fact takes place at the genital level," he observes drolly.[59] "Regarding the Jew, we think of money and its derivatives," he continues. "Regarding the black man, we think of sex."[60] The black man is consequently "attacked [once more] in his corporeality. It is his tangible personality that is lynched. It is his actual being that is dangerous."[61]

But culture and assimilation still mattered. "The black man is, in every sense of the word, a victim of white civilization," Fanon remarks. "Cultural imposition is easily at work in Martinique. . . . The real white man is waiting for me. He will tell me on the very first occasion that it is not enough for the intention to be white; whiteness has to be achieved in its totality."[62] However, Fanon also registers a critical ambivalence toward a separate black status, as determined by colonial rule and Négritude both. "What's all this about black people and a black nationality? I am

French," he categorically affirms at one point. "I am interested in French culture, French civilization, and the French. We refuse to be treated as outsiders; we are well and truly part of French history and its drama. . . . I take a personal interest in the destiny of France, the French nation, and its values. What am I supposed to do with a black empire?"[63]

These mercurial critical positions, expressed in both serious and acerbic tones, highlight Fanon's difficulty in finding resolution. Indeed, it must be emphasized that he does not call for the end of French rule, as he does so emphatically in his final book, *The Wretched of the Earth*. His positions mark a sharp internal critique, not an invocation of anticolonial revolution. He sought self-knowledge first; application could come later. Yet his final two chapters begin to outline a more concrete political program. "The black problem is not just about Blacks living among Whites, but about the black man exploited, enslaved, and despised by a colonialist and capitalist society that happens to be white," Fanon states in chapter 6.[64] A concrete set of socioeconomic class relations existed beneath the surface of racial difference. Addressing race alone was ultimately inadequate. In similar fashion, he is critical toward strictly philosophical self-knowledge, writing in one instance, "What is the point of meditating on Bantu ontology when we read elsewhere: 'When 75,000 black miners went on strike [in South Africa] in 1946, the state police forced them back to work with the barrel of the gun and bayonets. Twenty-five were killed and thousands

wounded."[65] Such oppression could not be passively received. "In every society, in every community, there exists,
must exist, a channel, an outlet whereby the energy accumulated in the form of aggressiveness can be released,"
Fanon asserts, calling this expression of energy, in a fore-
shadowing of his last book, a "collective catharsis."[66] In
these ways, Fanon ultimately sought action, rather than
critical deliberation alone.

## By Way of Conclusion

Yet the conclusion to *Black Skin, White Masks* ends on a
note of uncertainty once more, similar to that found in
the introduction. Its title, "By Way of Conclusion," indicates a temporary stopping point—the questions raised
remain unresolved, despite the extensive answers he
has provided. It is telling that the epigraph for this final
chapter is from *The Eighteenth Brumaire of Louis Bonaparte* (1852) by Karl Marx (1818–1883). It contrasts with
the introductory epigraph by Césaire, which cites a status
quo rather than looking toward the future. *Discourse on
Colonialism* and *The Eighteenth Brumaire* are both critical of centralized state power in the forms of European
colonialism and Bonapartism, respectively. Both are
critical of French politics specifically. But, more deeply,
the choice of this particular text by Marx seems cal-
culated, given its analysis of the 1848 Revolution, which
resulted in citizenship rights for Martinique, yet eventually the establishment of the Second Empire (1852–70).
Thus, in referencing this study, Fanon appears to be

repeating Marx's warning about the risks of revolution. Had Fanon cited *The Communist Manifesto* (1848), the message would have been far different.

As it stands, Fanon aligns himself with Marx, but conveys diffidence about what political revolution at the systemic level, whether constitutional (as in 1946) or anti-colonial, might bring—an ambivalence that contrasts with his later arguments. For Fanon at this early stage of his political thinking, transformation must begin, in classic psychiatric fashion, at the individual level. Indeed, Marx's text is arguably more *actional*, to use Fanon's term, than Césaire's. It contains two oft-quoted remarks: the first being that history repeats itself, "the first time as tragedy, the second as farce"; and the second being that "men make their own history, but they do not make it just as they please; they do not make it under circumstances chosen by themselves, but under circumstances directly encountered, given and transmitted from the past."[67] Fanon's critical departure from Césaire in the preceding chapters is therefore enabled further through Marx. "The social revolution cannot draw its poetry from the past, but only from the future. It cannot begin with itself before it has stripped itself of all its superstitions concerning the past," proposes Marx, as quoted by Fanon in his epigraph.[68]

The change Fanon envisions—societal in scope, but starting with the individual—cannot be drawn from history. He thus advocates a break from Négritude once more, from being "a slave to the past." In reference to

Césaire's epic poem, *Cahier d'un retour au pays natal*, and its grappling with Haiti, he is "not just responsible for the slave revolt in Saint Domingue."[69] "In no way does my basic vocation have to be drawn from the past of peoples of color," Fanon declares. "In no way do I have to dedicate myself to reviving a black civilization unjustly ignored. I will not make myself the man of any past. I do not want to sing the past to the detriment of my present and my future."[70] Indeed, in a moment indicative of his later identification with the Algerian cause, he cites the anti-colonial struggle then occurring in Vietnam as an example of this forward-looking stance: "The Vietnamese who die in front of a firing squad don't expect their sacrifice to revive a forgotten past. They accept death for the sake of the present and the future."[71] Still, Fanon recognized the difficulty of departing from history, given how it fixed his racial identity: "If the question once arose for me about showing solidarity with a given past, it was because I was committed to myself and my fellow man, to fight with all my life and all my strength so that never again would people be enslaved on this earth."[72] Yet he finds such recourse to be ultimately limiting, asking, in his inimitable, mordant tone, "Haven't I got better things to do on this earth than avenge the Blacks of the seventeenth century?"[73]

In the end, Fanon finds himself trapped—not by history, but by the racial subjection that fixed him to a particular history. It limited his French citizenship and its meanings, resulting in a hybrid citizen-subject status. "Here is my life caught in the noose of existence," he laments. "Here is my freedom, which sends back to me my own reflection."[74] He similarly stresses, "It is not the black world that governs my behavior. My black skin is not a repository for specific values."[75] But, in a return to existentialism, he pursues an abiding notion of free will, the possibility of achieving an authentic self. "I can also revise my past, prize it, or condemn it, depending on what I choose," he writes, pronouncing, "It is not my duty to be this or that."[76] As a consequence, he reserves his final critique for the reinforcement of racial difference by white and black alike. Fanon cites the pervasive risk of engaging in bad faith, a practice of self-deception, by embracing a "black soul" that is, as philosopher Kwame Anthony Appiah describes, a white construction of blackness.[77]

The illusion of racial difference, as with Négritude, and the superiority complex held by whites both needed to be forcefully confronted. The end of racism required deconstructing whiteness and blackness alike. "The black man is not. No more than the white man," Fanon concludes in one of his better-known statements, underscoring the mutually dehumanizing effects of racism.[78] Both blacks and whites need to "move away from the inhuman voices of their respective ancestors so that a genuine communication can be born. . . . It is through self-consciousness and renunciation, through a permanent tension of his freedom, that man can create the ideal conditions of existence for a human world."[79] Along with his oft-cited final prayer that he be a man who always questions, this last, profound appeal for a new humanism without the debilitating effects of racial difference ultimately reveals the deeper political aspiration, beyond the immediate circumstances of the Fourth Republic, that animates *Black Skin, White Masks.*

Yet the persistent difficulty of the book, which resides in Fanon's intellectual restlessness, his tonal shifts, and his refusal to base his argument on any single method or solution, has often mitigated this message. Indeed, this first work possesses clear weaknesses of repetition, obscurity, and incompletion—qualities that have undoubtedly encouraged the growth of a secondary literature to explain Fanon's objectives. *Black Skin, White Masks* goes in different directions and can be read in multiple ways, defying easy summary. Yet the book's pliable approach did not simply reflect the limitations of a first-time author. It was intentional. Fanon's technique embraced an ethos of moral resistance, outlining an internal civic critique from inside France.[80] His thinking emerged within this imperial space, unlike the postcolonial vantage point of Tunisia, where he composed *The Wretched of the Earth.* Still, this first work represents nothing less than an attempt at remapping racial understanding and a search for political progress and humane resolution—principles that would continue to inform Fanon's thought and movement for the rest of his life.

4

# Algeria

> The liberation of the Algerian national
> territory is a defeat for racism and for the
> exploitation of man; it inaugurates the
> unconditional reign of Justice.
> —*Toward the African Revolution*[1]

After *Black Skin, White Masks* garnered limited notice, Fanon's attention turned to securing a permanent position as a psychiatrist. Jobs were few, given that psychiatry was still a relatively unique specialization. Martinique offered little opportunity, a fact reinforced for Fanon by the difficulties his sister Gabrielle encountered as a pharmacist, despite her training in France. It must be emphasized, then, that his fortuitous acceptance of a position in Blida, Algeria, was the result of professional need, not political intention. Nevertheless, Algeria marked a turn in Fanon's career that unquestionably affected his thought and perspective in profound ways. It granted him a new place to think from, to confront the realities of French colonialism. His wartime experience in Algeria and his work with Algerian patients in France provided a

Map 4.1 Algeria circa 1950.

degree of familiarity with the social and cultural context to which he was moving. His article "The 'North African Syndrome,'" published in *Esprit* in February 1952, suggests the beginnings of a political empathy on the part of Fanon, by describing both the pejorative stereotypes French doctors used for Algerian patients and the psychosomatic illness Algerians suffered in France due to a "perpetual state of insecurity."[2] But Fanon's application to work there was a career choice, which aligned with a common pattern of imperial mobility.

Fanon lived and worked in Algeria from 1953 to 1956—only three years, despite his strong identification with the country. It proved long enough. The time between Fanon's arrival in Blida in October 1953 and the start of the Algerian war for independence was brief. The Algerian Revolution was among France's most prolonged decolonization struggles, lasting from 1954 to 1962. The Indochina War in Southeast Asia lasted a comparable length of time, from 1946 to 1954. The Algerian War began in November 1954, only months after the French defeat at Dien Bien Phu by the Viet Minh in north Vietnam—a siege from March to May 1954 that led to the Geneva Accords, which provided for the withdrawal of France from Indochina, where it had ruled since 1887.

The victory of a grassroots guerrilla army over the French proved highly symbolic, demonstrating that a strategy of anticolonial armed struggle could be successful. When Fanon returned to Algeria in 1953, he consequently entered a political crucible far different from the one he encountered during the Second World War. Indeed, given his political future, it remains a historical irony that Fanon's first experience in Algeria was in the service of liberating France from fascist foreign occupation. Parallels to colonial rule became transparent. Similar to Ahmed Ben Bella, the first president of independent Algeria, Fanon had been one of many colonial veterans who had fought for an empire that—contrary to promises of liberty, equality, and fraternity—restricted the meaning of citizenship rights and who, as a result, later fought against that very empire for independence.

This paradox of fighting against fascism while living under a kind of colonial fascism vitally informed Fanon's views, as it did political rhetoric more generally during this period, Aimé Césaire's *Discourse on Colonialism* being a paradigmatic example.[3] This contradiction also explains the timing of the Algerian nationalist movement's emergence. Anticolonial sentiments were long-held, and Algerian nationalism took shape over several decades. As the historian Martin Evans has written, Algerian politics had consisted of four competing strands: leftists, assimilationists, a religious clerical movement, and nationalists, "each of which looked beyond Algeria for inspiration."[4] But Algeria experienced a sharp rise in activism against French rule at the end of the Second World War with unrest starting in May 1945, the same month as the surrender of Nazi Germany. These protests were organized by the Association of the Friends of the Manifesto and Liberty (Association des Amis du Manifeste et de la Liberté or AML), founded in 1944, and the more radical Algerian People's Party (Parti du Peuple Algérien or PPA), established in 1937. The manifesto in question was the 1943 Manifesto of the Algerian People, an important document that called for the Algerian right to self-determination in place of a revised policy of assimilation that French officials had proposed to assuage local political ambitions. Algerian politics during the first half of the twentieth century resembled the politics found in other territories of the French Empire (and other empires), being animated by a tension between local, Western-educated elites, who held aspirations of equal citizenship, and a ruling government that sought to maintain hierarchical boundaries.[5] Long-standing ideas of racial and cultural difference played decisive roles in determining status, opportunity, and political grievance—a situation Fanon knew firsthand. Indeed, his experiences in France and Martinique as examined in *Black Skin, White Masks* prepared him for what he confronted in Algeria. Fanon was a foreign observer who quickly gained the empathy of a critic and activist. He was an itinerant intellectual who found an anticolonial struggle that resonated with his own experiences.

## Histories of Violence

In 1848 slavery ended in Martinique, the same year the French declared political control over Algeria—a coincidence partly reflecting geopolitical shifts that accompanied the 1848 revolutions that swept Europe. The French colonization of Algeria had begun in 1830, while the territory was still part of the Ottoman Empire. Algeria had drawn attention during the preceding centuries as a place along the Barbary Coast that provided safe haven for Berber pirates who disrupted trade in the Mediterranean. This persistent instability provided one motivation for seeking order during the nineteenth century. French racism and a budding "civilizing mission" (*mission civilisatrice*) further rationalized intervention. Considered liberal in his views on Algeria, Alexis de Tocqueville (1805–1859)—author of *Democracy in America*

(1835 and 1840) and, thus, an early interpreter (and apologist) for European settler colonialism—supported a limited form of colonization, professing in a report to the French National Assembly in 1847, "The Muslim society in North Africa was not uncivilised; it only had a backward and imperfect civilisation."[6]

The French did encounter strong resistance, particularly by Abd al-Qādir (1808–1883), a Muslim leader and scholar, who sought to build an Islamic state against French intrusion. A more robust military effort that ensued in 1841 established French rule in the north by 1848, with the three territories of Algiers, Oran, and Constantine becoming departments of France, similar to Martinique. However, this process of colonial military conquest was not completed until 1871—if it ever finished. Colonial violence continued, as did white settlement.

By 1889 French citizenship was extended to all European settlers, which included Spanish, Italians, and Maltese, while native Algerians remained colonial subjects (*indigènes*) under the *Code de l'indigénat* (1865), unless they assimilated to French culture. This option for naturalized citizenship meant relinquishing Islam in particular—an impossible choice for many. Despite French citizenship status, white settlers—popularly known as *pieds-noirs* ("black feet")—were situated existentially between metropolitan French citizens and Algerian colonial subjects. They distinguished themselves in spirit from the former, while being racist toward the latter. Over time, many pieds-noirs would never live in France. The settler community would remain significantly outnumbered, with a figure of only 1 million compared to 9 million Algerians in 1954.[7] Yet this settler population accrued significant political clout in the decades ahead.[8]

World War I proved to be a crucial turning point for Algerian politics, as elsewhere in the colonial world. The end of the war witnessed the establishment of the League of Nations in 1920 as a new international institution in world politics, with expressed concern for the "just treatment" of colonial peoples as listed in Article 23 of the Covenant of the League. More influential was the right to self-determination initiated in U.S. president Woodrow Wilson's Fourteen Points speech delivered in 1918. Though the term *self-determination* did not appear in his address, Point Five stressed that the interests of colonial subject populations be given "equal weight" in matters of determining sovereignty. Immediately preceding this emergent trend in world politics had been the recruitment of colonial subjects to fight in the war. Approximately 170,000 Algerians served, with many expecting citizenship rights and benefits for their military service—a popular demand that intersected with the interests of *évolués,* an elite class of Algerians, similar to that found in Martinique, who had assimilated into French culture through language, education, and profession. However, as with the factor of race, which created a treacherous boundary between *évolués* and white French citizens in places like the Antilles, Islam marked an additional cultural difference that rationalized discriminatory treatment on the part of the French government, despite assimilationist principles to the contrary.

These limitations generated pressures for reform, in addition to fomenting proto-nationalist movements that were anticolonial in orientation. Taking a stance of accommodation, the Federation of Elected Natives (Fédération des Élus Indigènes), founded in 1926, sought full citizenship for *évolués*, regardless of religion. On the other hand, the more radical Star of North Africa (Étoile Nord-Africaine), also established in 1926, sought complete political independence for Algeria. Ahmed Ben Messali Hadj (1898–1974), a founder and dominant figure in the latter movement, would go on to start the nationalist PPA, cited earlier. Messali Hadj attended the famous League against Imperialism meeting in Brussels, Belgium, in 1927, where he met Ho Chi Minh (1890–1969), the future leader of the Viet Minh, among other activists—a vital occasion that highlighted the broader world of anticolonial politics then emerging. Messali Hadj gradually moved away from leftist politics to embrace an Arab-Islamic nationalist identity. He is widely considered to be the father of Algerian nationalism.

What is important to understand in revisiting the interwar period is that nationalism in Algeria took root well before the Algerian Revolution. Moreover, it did not manifest fully formed. Rather, it was the result of a layered history of political activism, divided between amending French rule and overthrowing it. French response to these early efforts heightened tensions. The rise of anticolonial politics generated an official policy known as the Blum-Viollette Plan (1936), named after a former French governor, Maurice Viollette (1870–1960), which further opened citizenship to educated Algerians. The plan proved to be controversial—supported by some Algerians, while viewed by others as separating elites (and, thus, a potential revolutionary vanguard) from the colonial masses, resulting in a divide-and-rule strategy. French settlers also took a critical stance, perceiving the plan as a first step toward permitting the Arab-Muslim majority to overtake their entrenched minority power. The reintroduction of reform after the Second World War generated a more critical Algerian response, with prior supporters like Ferhat Abbas (1899–1985), who founded the AML, advocating greater autonomy for Algeria within a possible federation with France. Messali Hadj, then under house arrest in France, continued a more radical stance through the PPA, arguing for complete independence.[9]

These differences among Algerian leaders attained urgency after the protests of May 1945 that resulted in violence by the French military—a crackdown known as the Sétif Massacre, named after the Algerian town where it occurred. As described by Alistair Horne, whose book *A Savage War of Peace* (1977) remains a classic account of the Algerian Revolution, Sétif had a deep history of anticolonial sentiment, and the march staged on May 8—V.E. Day, marking the surrender of Nazi Germany—underscored connections between antifascism and long-brewing anticolonial tensions.[10] Though debate exists as to who started the violence, the estimated 8,000 Algerian activists who had gathered eventually turned on French settlers, killing 103 and wounding 100 more. The French response was brutal, involving executions and aerial bombing—a strategy known as *ratissage* ("raking over"). Mortality estimates range from 1,300 (an official French figure) to 45,000 Algerians (a figure reported by Egypt and embraced by Algerians).[11] Fanon himself would later cite 45,000 victims.[12] While these demonstrations originated partly due to wartime conditions of scarcity and unemployment, they nevertheless received support from the PPA and its broader aspiration for independence.

The massacre in turn spurred a reorganization of Algerian politics. The AML was banned, with Abbas founding the Democratic Union of the Algerian Manifesto (Union Démocratique du Manifeste Algérien or UDMA) in its wake. Messali Hadj returned from exile to start the Movement for the Triumph of Democratic Liberties (Mouvement pour le Triomphe des Libertés Démocratiques), essentially a new version of the PPA, which also continued and whose military offshoot, the Organisation Spéciale (OS), initiated a strategy of armed struggle in 1947. It provided a path for the ascendance of Ahmed Ben Bella. Ben Bella participated in the OS and later helped establish the Revolutionary Committee of Unity and Action (Comité Révolutionnaire pour l'Unité et l'Action or CRUA) in 1954 while in exile in Cairo, following the dissolution of the OS in 1951. The CRUA evolved into the National Liberation Front (Front de Libération Nationale or FLN), the nationalist organization that would become central to the revolution and that Fanon would support until the end of his life.

Inspired by the French defeat at Dien Bien Phu the previous May, the war started on November 1, 1954, when FLN fighters launched a series of attacks referred to by the French as the *Toussaint Rouge,* since it occurred on All Saints' Day. While its coordination of multiple assaults displayed an audacity that announced the FLN's presence and intentions, popular support for the FLN gained traction only gradually. As David Macey has written, "There was little or no reason to suspect in November 1954 that a war of national liberation had begun in Algeria, that it would bring down the Fourth French Republic, return de Gaulle to power in 1958 and bring with it the threat of a military coup in France itself. There was no reason to suspect that over one million French troops, the majority of them very young conscripts, would serve in Algeria or that over 27,000 of them would die there in the war with no name."[13] Though the FLN had little early success, the French government and local pieds-noirs, who eventually faced a choice between "the suitcase and the coffin," soon responded in force.[14]

French brutality can partly be attributed to the violent crackdown in Madagascar (1947–48) and, especially, the loss of Indochina—a humiliating defeat, as perceived by the French public, and one to avoid repeating. In fact, many French soldiers who had fought there served in Algeria. As one sign of this shame, the historian Fredrik Logevall has estimated that 110,000 French troops and imperial auxiliaries died in Southeast Asia—a starkly higher figure than the eventual French death toll in Algeria, albeit a much lower figure than the 200,000 soldiers the Viet Minh lost, with at least as many Vietnamese civilians killed.[15] But an independent Algeria was also unimaginable, since Algeria was legally a part of France since 1881—the Mediterranean flowing through a "Greater France" similar to the Seine flowing through Paris.[16] This perspective also meant the conflict was understood to be domestic in scope—an internal matter, unlike Vietnam—and the Geneva Conventions (last ratified in 1949) that protected the rights of combatants and noncombatants in times of war did not apply. However, though police were initially involved through Operation Bitter Orange, military operations soon followed.

By April 1955 a state of emergency was declared. Given the unconventional nature of the FLN and its guerrilla tactics, thousands of Algerians were arrested. Torture became a common technique of interrogation for information about the FLN. Beatings, suffocation, bodily suspension, electrical shocks, and rape were employed by French authorities. By May 100,000 French soldiers had been deployed and a year later, in April 1956, another 200,000 joined their ranks. This magnitude enabled the pursuit of a strategy of *quadrillages* (quadrants) that dispersed small military units across the country to maintain control. In contrast to earlier operations of *ratissage* that sought reprisal against insurgents, this approach sought stability: a uniform French presence. It also left French units vulnerable to attack. Large battles proved rare. The FLN and its armed wing, the National Liberation Army (Armée de Libération Nationale or ALN), preferred ambush as a primary tactic.

The Philippeville massacres in August 1955, which resulted in the death of 71 Europeans and at least 1,200—and possibly as many as 12,000—Algerians, marked a key turning point after ten months, with reconciliation of any sort appearing more remote.[17] The FLN/ALN indicated that it could be as brutal as the French, embracing a strategy of total war that targeted civilians. It also became clear that the FLN had auxiliary support from Tunisia, which had gained self-government that June and would become independent in March 1956. Among those distraught by the escalating violence, Albert Camus—a pied-noir himself, albeit a more progressive one as, briefly, a member of the Algerian Communist Party and a sometime supporter of Messali Hadj and the PPA—called for a "civil truce" in January 1956. He organized a public meeting that included Ferhat Abbas and advocated the protection of civilian noncombatants. But Camus's idealism faced sharp criticism from all sides, including the pied-noir community.[18] Abbas and the UDMA threw their support behind the FLN, which Abbas would later help lead from Tunis beginning in 1958. Messali Hadj did not back the FLN and started a competing armed front, the Algerian

National Movement (Mouvement National Algérien), which gradually led to his marginalization. However, a second important shift soon followed—the Soummam Conference of August 1956, during which FLN leaders, headed by Abane Ramdane (1920–1957), created the National Council of the Algerian Revolution (Conseil National de la Révolution Algérienne), a new representative governing body to be based in Cairo.[19]

Though the war had had an international character from its inception, the Soummam Conference formalized such an approach, by approving the extension of conflict to France itself as well as seeking support across North Africa and elsewhere in the emerging Third World. Positioning the FLN as the sole representative of the Algerian cause, the 1956 Soummam Declaration identified the Algerian Revolution ideologically as nationalist and secular and demographically as racially and culturally heterogeneous—two key measures. In the words of the declaration itself, "The Algerian Revolution wishes to conquer national independence in order to establish a democratic and social republic guaranteeing true equality to all citizens of the same country, without discrimination."[20] Following on proclamations made in November 1954 and April 1955, this bolder statement clarified the intentions of the FLN in order to blunt French attempts to categorize its activities as terrorism and the result of Islamic militancy. The FLN had a distinct and comprehensive program of national liberation. Indeed, the Soummam Declaration and Abane, who was one of the

architects of the Battle of Algiers (1956–57), had a profound impact on Fanon and his political thinking. Fanon
identified with a specific political platform within the
FLN. Alice Cherki has written that Fanon "felt a special
connection" to Abane and "saw him as a true revolutionary leader of the new Algeria."[21] The fighting in Algeria
was not a civil war or a religious war, but an anticolonial
war. The once domestic nature of the conflict was trans-
forming into a total nationalist struggle.[22]

Following this bold political announcement, the FLN
audaciously moved its strategy of armed confrontation
to Algeria's capital city. The notorious Battle of Algiers
formally started in September 1956. It consisted of sabotage, bombing, and hit-and-run assassinations by the
FLN/ALN, matched by torture and other counterinsurgency measures by the French. It was a gruesome conflict,
later vividly fictionalized by Italian film director Gillo
Pontecorvo (1919–2006) in *The Battle of Algiers* (1966),
based on a memoir by Saadi Yacef (1928–present), an
FLN leader in Algiers, titled *Souvenirs de la Bataille d'Alger*
(1962). These tactics on the part of the FLN/ALN and
the French alike enhanced the dirty character of the war,
with civilians being targeted once more for support and
elimination by both sides. But the conflict had escalated
more generally, with approximately 450,000 French soldiers in Algeria—a 1957 estimate, up from only 57,000
in November 1954—against 40,000 ALN fighters (a 1957
estimate).[23] As described by Horne, ALN forces peaked
in 1958, with French assessments suggesting 60,000 total

(regular and irregular) soldiers and the FLN claiming over 100,000 fighters.[24] An additional 79,000 Algerians (a 1958 estimate)—including 60,000 known as the Harkis—also served in the French army, a loyalism that would result in internecine strife during and after the war.[25]

Overall, this complex situation of violence, competing political affiliations, and the overriding question of self-determination would preoccupy Fanon and his writing on the conflict in the years ahead. The war resisted easy analysis. It defied the colonial Manichaeism that Fanon had identified and interrogated in his first book.

## Blida

Blida, the town where Fanon took up his new position, was only fifty kilometers (approximately thirty-one miles) from Algiers. It was segregated like most urban areas at the time, between an affluent section for *colons* (settlers) and a poorer Arab quarter. Describing what Fanon encountered, Cherki writes that Algerian society had "for a long time been structured and compartmentalized, almost branded into its three major components: Europeans, Jews, and natives, which is to say Christians, Jews, and Muslims."[26] But Blida was equally a place of natural beauty, sitting at the foot of the Atlas Mountains. It was also known as Algeria's "capital of madness."[27]

The Hôpital Psychiatrique de Blida-Joinville (HPB) that Fanon joined was the largest psychiatric hospital in North Africa. After initial planning in 1912, it was constructed during the late 1920s and accepted patients starting in 1933, officially opening in 1938. The HPB specialized in treating curable ailments—that is, it did not permanently institutionalize patients. Though it had only seven hundred beds, it served up to fifteen hundred people shortly after its opening. The majority of those treated were Algerian, with four doctors administering care.[28] Fanon filled a fifth position.[29] Richard Keller, in a recent history of psychiatry in French North Africa, has written that the Blida facility had over two thousand patients at the time of the Algerian War—a sign of its popular use and its continued, though overcrowded, role during the conflict.[30] In fact, Fanon and the other four physicians petitioned French authorities on the need for improved facilities.[31] Though debate over funding and medical technique characterized its existence, the HPB served as a prime symbol of the French civilizing mission in North Africa, given its dispensation of modern medical treatment.

The practice of psychiatry frequently collaborated with colonial endeavors—not only in the French Empire, but across the imperial world.[32] Rudimentary mental institutions existed during the nineteenth century, though formal psychiatric hospitals were not widespread until the early twentieth century. Remarkably, legislation passed as early as 1838 entailing every French *département* to provide mental health facilities.[33] These nascent efforts, however, amounted to little more than prisons. As in other cases of the civilizing mission, paradoxes emerged. On the one hand, a sense of benevolence existed to aid the mentally ill among the colonized. French psychiatrists believed they were "liberating" such patients from their ailments, citing as a role model Philippe Pinel (1745–1826), who sought the humane treatment of those deemed insane during the French Revolution.[34] On the other hand, these intentions were deeply informed by cultural and racial biases. Attempts at assessing the moral traits and psychology of "the Arab" had existed since the nineteenth century—a vital aspect of rationalizing colonial rule and the hierarchical differences between Western and Islamic civilizations. Indeed, the Arab mind and Islamic civilization were perceived as irrational, even unknowable, at a certain level. Yet doctors were encouraged to learn Arabic to improve their interaction with patients. Stereotypes of Arabs as passive, lazy, and childlike, but also pathologically violent, fanatical, and superstitious, similarly reinforced the idea that Algerians were beyond medical help. Still, Algerians and other colonial subjects were also understood to be treatable.[35]

These contradictory notions informed psychiatric care at the HPB. Medicine was not a neutral form of knowledge, despite scientific claims to the contrary. Treatments actively shaped, and were shaped by, colonialism. "Introduced into Algeria at the same time as racialism and humiliation, Western medical science, being part of the oppressive system, has always provoked in the native an ambivalent attitude," Fanon later writes in *A Dying Colonialism*.[36] The colonial version of psychiatric practice in Algeria became known as the Algiers School, which positioned the North African Arab between the "civilized" European and the "primitive" black African.[37] The key figure in this school was Antoine Porot (1876–1965), who headed the HPB. Fanon worked under him and would later critique the school in *The Wretched of the Earth*.[38] Yet, as Keller argues, Fanon must be understood as one voice among many that critiqued the racism of colonial psychiatry in North Africa.[39]

Still, as recounted by Cherki, who knew Fanon in Blida beginning in 1955, the HPB was "radically transformed by Fanon's arrival" due to his commitment to the humane sociotherapy model he learned at Saint-Alban.[40] Fanon worked with 187 patients initially, of whom 165 were European women. The remaining 22 were Algerian men, though Fanon did not speak Arabic.[41] Departing from existing practices at Blida, Fanon applied an innovative sociotherapeutic method with weekly meetings and events designed to create a sense of community. Films, music, a newspaper, and occupational therapy combined with traditional therapeutic and medical treatments provided a holistic approach to care. However, these methods had less impact on the Algerian men than on the European women—a situation of cultural difference and naiveté on the part of Fanon. He quickly readjusted. Activities were revised to account for gender-appropriate forms of occupational therapy as well as local cultural practices, such as Friday prayers and traditional religious holidays. "It was not simply a matter of imposing imported methods that had been more or less adapted to the *native mentality,*" Fanon reportedly explained, in defense of his techniques. "I needed to have the support of the Algerian staff in order to incite them to rebel against the prevailing method, to make them realize that their competence was equal to that of the Europeans. The burden of suggesting appropriate forms of socialization and integrating them into the sociotherapy process had to be placed on the Algerian staff. That's what happened. Psychiatry . . . has to be political."[42]

To improve his experimental approach, Fanon made trips in the area surrounding Blida to gain a more intimate and empathetic sense of local cultural life.[43] Indeed, Fanon's life blossomed in Algeria. Joby Fanon has recalled his brother having a comfortable home there with Josie, mixing work and play, trips to the beaches of the Mediterranean, and, eventually, the birth of Fanon's son, Olivier, in 1955.[44] Yet this budding tranquility was cut short by the war. Blida was removed from much of the Algerian conflict until 1956. But French patrols had been attacked, and acts of sabotage had occurred in the area.[45] The Algerian struggle ultimately proved unavoidable.

Fanon's path to supporting the Algerian cause and joining the FLN can be described as both gradual and instantly foreseeable in retrospect, given his preexisting political, as well as medical, commitments. His first contact with activists was in 1955 through Amitiés Algériennes, a humanitarian organization, though Fanon had worked, and had a strong rapport, with Algerian student interns, who sympathized with the FLN.[46] He encountered the war principally through the context of the HPB, where he witnessed firsthand the effects of violence and torture—medical cases that would make their way into *The Wretched of the Earth*. Admitted patients included both victims and perpetrators, on French and Algerian sides alike. Known by then for his criticism of colonial psychiatry, Fanon provided medical help for the FLN after being approached, in addition to sheltering its guerrillas at the hospital and within his own home.[47] The dangers involved in this decision must not be taken lightly. As David Macey has written, the situation became extraordinarily precarious, with Fanon vulnerable to French arrest as well as FLN suspicion early on.[48]

Fanon eventually received anonymous death threats and survived a bomb explosion outside his home, a state of affairs that led to his resignation from Blida and his departure with his family from Algeria in December 1956. Indeed, he was formally expelled, following his letter of resignation from the HPB. But other FLN activists were leaving as well.[49] The Battle of Algiers had started, and the war of liberation was escalating. In his letter of resignation, Fanon expressed his devotion to the hospital, but the situation in Algeria had become untenable. "Madness is one of the ways in which man can lose his freedom. And being placed at this intersection, I can say that I have come to realize with horror how alienated the inhabitants of this country are," Fanon wrote. "If psychiatry is a medical technique which aspires to allow man to cease being alienated from his environment, I owe it to myself to assert that the Arab, who is permanently alienated in his own country, lives in a state of absolute depersonalization. The status of Algeria? Systematic dehumanization. . . . For long months, my conscience has been the seat of unforgiveable debates. And their conclusion is a will not to lose hope in man, or in other words myself."[50] In characteristic fashion, his letter, initiated by personal circumstances, reaches for a broader context and meaning—a self-awareness of the history shaping his life once more, and a need to find a more effective response, beyond his current position and abilities.

5

# Tunisia

Algeria is virtually independent. The Algerians
already consider themselves sovereign.
It remains for France to recognize her.
—*A Dying Colonialism*[1]

Fanon departed Algeria in late December 1956, never to
live there again. Despite his strong association with the
country, he spent just over three years at Blida. He resided
longer in Tunisia, which had become independent from
France in March 1956. Fanon also left behind his professional life as he knew it. Though he found a position
as a psychiatrist in Tunis, he committed himself more
fully to the Algerian cause, as well as his political writing.[2] Indeed, his move from Algeria to Tunisia marked
his transition from committing acts of escalating civil
disobedience to openly promoting total political revolution. Removed from immediate surroundings of war and
surveillance, Fanon found greater freedom to express his
support, without the constant threat of arrest. He had
actively helped the FLN through medical assistance at
Blida, but his writing had been more muted vis-à-vis the

struggle—a state of affairs seen in his paper "Racism and Culture" delivered at the First World Congress of Black Writers and Artists, sponsored by *Présence africaine,* in Paris in September 1956. Though provocative, Fanon's presentation gestured only obliquely toward the anti-colonial war in Algeria.[3]

Algeria itself had grown increasingly isolated. Like Tunisia, its neighbor Morocco also achieved independence from France in 1956. A number of African colonies still remaining under French rule—including Senegal, Mali, Niger, Chad, Gabon, Madagascar, Togo, Cameroon, Benin, Burkina Faso, Côte d'Ivoire (Ivory Coast), the Central African Republic, Mauritania, and the Republic of the Congo (Congo-Brazzaville)—would later become independent in 1960, the "Year of Africa," named for this sweeping change.

The independence and political stance of African countries beyond the French Empire mattered as well. Decolonization in Francophone sub-Saharan Africa was preceded by the independence of Ghana (previously the British Gold Coast) in 1957, with President Kwame Nkrumah (1909–1972) seeking a pan-African revival across the continent for the postcolonial period. Egypt, under the equally charismatic leadership of Gamal Abdel Nasser (1918–1970), also emerged as a vital regional player and supporter of the FLN and pan-Arabism more generally, particularly after the 1956 Suez Crisis, when Britain and France failed to retake control of the Suez Canal after Nasser nationalized it for Egypt. Further change continued apace with the Mau Mau Uprising in Kenya, an anticolonial struggle that approximated Algeria's as the British employed internment camps and torture to brutally suppress dissent. South African activists of the African National Congress, the South African Communist Party, and the Pan Africanist Congress also turned away from strategies of nonviolent protest, believing that only armed resistance could overthrow the racist apartheid regime that had been established in 1948. This sentiment took hold particularly after the Sharpeville Massacre in 1960, when police killed sixty-nine antigovernment protesters. Like Algeria, Kenya and South Africa both possessed recalcitrant white communities that made fundamental political reform unlikely. White minority rule would not be relinquished without a fight.

These political developments across Africa profoundly affected Fanon, expanding his political horizon beyond Algeria. Indeed, his time in Tunisia was essential in broadening his thinking. If Algeria provided a place in which he could observe the broader effects of French colonialism, Tunisia provided a new postcolonial vantage point from which he could begin to draw more general conclusions. Though French Algeria grew isolated, the FLN continued to internationalize its cause following the 1956 Soummam Conference, a strategy Fanon embraced. It was consequently an intense and productive period defined by writing and diplomatic travel to Europe and other parts of Africa, in addition to medical work that continued to involve Algerian patients. Except for a brief interval in 1960, when he served as an FLN diplomat in Accra, Tunisia would remain his primary residence for the next five years. Like Egypt and Morocco, Tunisia served as an indispensable ally for the FLN, providing shelter for a number of Algerian activists and refugees, with as many as 150,000 Algerians there during the war.[4] Within this context of proximity and refuge, Fanon's perspectives on violence and popular struggle gestated, eventually resulting in his polemic of anticolonial revolution, *The Wretched of the Earth.*

But his political journalism for the FLN publication *El Moudjahid* and his short book of essays *A Dying Colonialism* (1959) proved imperative for his intellectual evolution between the cerebral *Black Skin, White Masks* and its more programmatic successor.[5] Often underestimated, these intermediate writings deserve equal attention. Ato Sekyi-Otu has insisted that Fanon's texts be read "*dialectically* rather than *sequentially* or as discrete entities."[6] Though his books should not be read in isolation, and cannot be fully understood by simply reading them chronologically, engaging them in order of publication does usefully illuminate Fanon's apprenticeship as a writer—the ways in which each book progressively refined his thinking, the intellectual cul-de-sacs he left behind, and the increasing political ambitions and constraints he experienced that both limited and advanced his productivity. His transformation in Tunisia into a full-time activist-intellectual and diplomat not only sharpened his political views; it focused his writing. Rather than addressing a select audience familiar with trends in philosophy and psychology as well as the French colonial situation, as found in the eclectic erudition of *Black Skin, White Masks,* Fanon embraced the task of speaking for a national cause and motivating a popular readership—urgent considerations that enhanced his existing skills of critical analysis and empathetic expression.

### El Moudjahid

The fall of 1956 and the spring of 1957 marked a critical period for the FLN. The initial period of revolutionary momentum would subside, a consequence of French counterinsurgency efforts and internal strife within the FLN leadership. In 1956 the FLN mounted repeated attacks against supporters of Messali Hadj, known as the Messalists, and his rival organization, the Mouvement National Algérien.[7] The Battle for Algiers also came to an end by March 1957—a defeat for the FLN—through the assassination and capture of important FLN leaders by the French. Equally damaging, Ben Bella and several other members of the FLN leadership were arrested in October 1956 via a plane hijacked by the French, en route from Rabat, Morocco, to Tunis. Ben Bella would remain in prison for the duration of the war. With the dissolution of the FLN's strategy in urban areas and the imprisonment of key officials, the FLN's activities became increasingly international in scope through the fact of exile, thus fulfilling, if by force of circumstance, one of the tenets of its original proclamation of November 1,

Figure 5.1 Frantz Fanon (*second row, center*) and hospital staff in Tunis, date unknown. *Permission granted and copyright owned by Fonds Frantz Fanon/IMEC.*

1954, which declared the "internationalization of the Algerian question" and the "realization of North African unity in its natural Arab-Muslim framework" among its main objectives.[8]

More marginal than these senior figures, Fanon nevertheless participated in this internationalization process. He had secured a position as a psychiatrist in Tunis at the Manouba Hospital, working once more with ALN fighters as well as Algerian refugees (figure 5.1).[9] He also pursued research for several scientific publications and even undertook clinical trial testing of a new medication, meprobamate, which was promoted as a tranquilizer. But Fanon became equally committed to *El Moudjahid* (*The Holy Revolutionary*), the main periodical of the FLN.

He joined its staff in June 1957 through his friendship with Abane Ramdane, whom he first met in Algeria in December 1956. This position not only formalized his membership in the FLN but groomed him to be one of its central spokesmen.[10] *El Moudjahid* appeared twice a month starting in 1957, with as many as 10,000 copies per issue.[11] Fanon worked directly with Redha Malek (1931–present), the general editor, and M'Hamed Yazid (1923–2003), a minister of information for the FLN.

Despite its status as the FLN's signature publication, *El Moudjahid* faced distinct challenges. As an organ of propaganda, its circulation was haphazard and often restricted, as its distribution or possession presented a risk for FLN members and supporters. Though published in French and Arabic editions, it nonetheless had a limited audience, given that many Algerians were illiterate—one effect of colonialism. David Macey reports the astonishing statistic that "in 1954, 86 per cent of Algerian men and 95 per cent of Algerian women could not read."[12] Radio broadcasts from Tunisia, Morocco, and Egypt— particularly Radio Cairo—therefore played a more vital role, a fact Fanon himself observed.[13]

But *El Moudjahid* remained important despite these constraints. Its pages did not exclusively contain journalism in the sense of firsthand reportage, but often interpretations of events intended to convert international readers and political leaders, not simply Algerians, into supporters of the FLN cause. Fanon's status as a foreigner and his cosmopolitan experience up to that point were useful in this regard, for the French edition and its intended readership. Yet it is important to stress that the articles in its pages reflected the work of an editorial team.[14] While the journalism collected in part 4 of *Toward the African Revolution* (1964) is attributed to Fanon, it must be understood as bearing the imprint of an editorial process designed to reflect the general views and positions of the FLN.[15] Still, these contributions, originally published from September 1957 to January 1960, encompass a spectrum of themes that reveal Fanon's experience of the Algerian War, his criticism of the French government and French intellectuals alike, and his thoughts on the decolonization of Africa then occurring.

Early pieces from 1957, such as "Disappointments and Illusions of French Colonialism" and "Algeria Face to Face with the French Torturers," undertake a responsive approach: explaining the FLN and its ambitions, the reasons for its struggle, and the pathological violence of French colonialism.[16] "Torture in Algeria is not an accident, or an error, or a fault," Fanon writes at one point in the second essay. "Colonialism cannot be understood without the possibility of torturing, of violating, or of massacring."[17] The issue of torture became a rallying point of international criticism, further exposed by the publication of *The Question* (1958) by French-Algerian journalist Henri Alleg (1921–2013), which detailed his own experience of being arrested and tortured by French paratroopers.

But beyond this anticipated critique, special malice was directed toward the French Left and its failure to

support the Algerian struggle thus far, a view that crys-
tallized for Fanon during a brief stay in France while in
transit between Blida and Tunis. As he discovered, leftist intellectuals were more preoccupied with the Soviet
invasion of Hungary in November 1956, which crushed
a popular revolt there. Even worse, in March 1956, the
French Communist Party had supported special measures in Algeria that effectively sanctioned martial law
to suppress anticolonial activism.[18] "Fanon no longer
thought, as he had previously, that the Socialists and
Communists were going to bring the war to an end. He
became increasingly aware of their inability to envisage
Algeria as an independent nation," Alice Cherki writes.
"The three years he spent in Algeria had convinced him
otherwise, and he was persuaded that independence was
the only possible outcome. He was already deeply committed to the Algerian resistance and considered himself
an insider."[19]

This disenchantment translated into a three-part
article in *El Moudjahid* titled "French Intellectuals and
Democrats and the Algerian Revolution" (1957). It accused leftist intellectuals of being patronizing toward
Algerian activists, ignorant of actual conditions, and
subject to political oscillation to the point of hypoc-
risy—supporting self-determination in principle, but
unable to imagine France fully relinquishing its ties
with Algeria. As historian James Le Sueur has argued,
Fanon highlighted a tacit Eurocentrism among French
intellectuals, how the appearance of political solidarity

hid continued forms of French paternalism, and how the French continued to betray their own revolutionary ideals established over a century and a half earlier. In Le Sueur's words, Fanon depicted them as unable to "struggle against their own state."[20]

Though these critical preoccupations toward the French would persist, Fanon's writing turned to other vistas as well, particularly those regarding transformations on the African continent. From 1958 forward, a wider engagement surfaced in his journalism, involving references to the Maghreb context of the war through the regional participation of Tunisia and Morocco, the continental implications of the Algerian struggle, and the broader landscape of international Cold War politics then being established.[21] Indeed, Fanon began to travel more at this time in the capacity of a diplomat representing the FLN, acquiring a Tunisian passport in 1958 that named him "Omar Ibrahim Fanon" originally from Tunis, effectively renouncing his French citizenship (figure 5.2). His diplomacy reflected both the ALN's setbacks in 1956 and 1957—namely, the French victory in the Battle of Algiers—and the subsequent turn toward further internationalization with the 1958 establishment of the Provisional Government of the Republic of Algeria (GPRA), a move intended to legitimize the FLN within the international community through a new institutional structure for political recognition. Armed struggle alone could not defeat the French. Diplomacy might.[22]

Figure 5.2 Frantz Fanon (*third from left*) and FLN/ALN leaders in Oudja, Morocco, late 1950s. The exact date is unconfirmed but is likely 1959, when Fanon is known to have visited Morocco. The persons to his left and right are also unconfirmed, though it is possible the man to his immediate right is Houari Boumédiène (1932–1978), who was stationed at Oudja and later succeeded Ben Bella as president of Algeria. The person to Fanon's far right is possibly Krim Belkacem (1922–1970), who served as a minister of defense and foreign minister within the GPRA. *Permission granted and copyright owned by Fonds Frantz Fanon/IMEC.*

This diplomatic turn paralleled the formation of a new French government by Charles de Gaulle. De Gaulle rose to power following the collapse of the Fourth Republic, which broke down as a result of growing dissent over Algeria.[23] Yet, despite the potential threat posed by this government, the GPRA received diplomatic recognition from a number of African and Asian countries, perhaps China most significantly. A Third World bloc had emerged since the start of the revolution—particularly with the 1955 Asian-African

Conference held in Bandung, Indonesia, which an FLN delegation attended unofficially. This conference had influenced the internationalism of the Soummam Declaration, and its emergent Third Worldism supported the Algerian cause as another struggle against the remnants of Western imperial rule in Africa and Asia.[24] "From Bandung to Cairo to Accra, all the Afro-Asiatic peoples, all the oppressed of yesterday bear, support, and increasingly assume the cause of the Algerian Revolution," Fanon contended, citing the significance of the Bandung meeting. "It is absolutely not exaggerated to say that, more and more, France will have two continents against her in Algeria."[25]

Fanon, however, equally anticipated emerging dangers—specifically neocolonialism in its different guises. The old formula of "Africa, France's restricted hunting ground" was gradually being superseded.[26] Attentive to a set of Cold War politics that was quickly reshaping a receding imperial landscape, Fanon noted how the United States, while distancing itself from France, sought to orchestrate this new order of great power influence. In his article "Letter to the Youth of Africa" (1958), Fanon further warned of African leaders who sought to negotiate with colonial powers, rather than commence struggle. With the proposal of a new French Community conceived by de Gaulle to replace the French Union (established in 1946) on the immediate political horizon in September 1958, Fanon accused Felix Houphouët-Boigny (1905–1993), future president of Côte d'Ivoire, of playing "the role of straw-man for French colonialism.

. . . Mr. Houphouët-Boigny has become the traveling salesman of French colonialism and he has not feared to appear before the United Nations to defend the French thesis."[27] Houphouët-Boigny had promoted a continued relationship between France and Francophone Africa. Fanon's turn against certain African elites—specifically those Francophone African leaders, including Léopold Senghor, who joined the French Community following the referendum in September 1958—prefigures later arguments found in *The Wretched of the Earth.*

Indeed, several essays from 1958 that are more conceptual in focus indicate Fanon's search for a programmatic take on what should be done. "In the course of the struggle for liberation, things are not clear in the consciousness of the fighting people," Fanon observes in one essay. "Since it [the struggle] is a refusal, at one and the same time, of political non-existence, of wretchedness, of illiteracy, of the inferiority complex so subtly instilled by oppression, its battle is for a long time undifferentiated. Neo-colonialism takes advantage of this indetermination."[28] He later writes after the French referendum and Guinea's refusal to join the community—resulting in its independence on September 30, 1958, under the leadership of Sékou Touré (1922–1984), whom Fanon greatly admired—that the "struggle against colonialism, in its specific aspect of exploitation of man by man, thus belongs in the general process of man's liberation."[29]

These incipient positions outline an increasingly ambitious sensibility, a need for clarity, and a renewed pursuit of universal meaning, beyond the FLN's aspirations in Algeria. They gesture toward a common purpose and future for the postcolonial world. In Fanon's words, through the Bandung pact, the "advent of peoples, unknown only yesterday, onto the stage of history" with "their determination to participate in the building of a civilization that has its place in the world of today" have granted vital importance and energy to "the world process of humanization."[30] *Black Skin, White Masks* critiqued Martinique and France. Fanon's essays for *El Moudjahid* captured a broader vision of the French Empire in decline. These evolving arguments that signaled an expanding political geography and the liberation of humanity—not just Algeria—as an aim would gain further momentum in Fanon's attendance at the All-African Peoples' Conference in Accra, Ghana, in December 1958—an event that marked his first diplomatic trip south of the Sahara, introducing him to a nascent postcolonial world, an emergent pan-Africanism, and a wider audience for popularizing armed struggle.[31]

### A Dying Colonialism

Given the unsigned nature of articles in *El Moudjahid*, *A Dying Colonialism* (1959)—originally titled *Year Five of the Algerian Revolution* (*L'An V de la Révolution algérienne*) and first translated into English as *Studies in a Dying Colonialism* (1965)—provided Fanon with greater public recognition as a key spokesman for the Algerian struggle. The difference in titles is notable. Though the war would last three more years, the English versions, translated after his death, impart optimism that French colonialism in Algeria was reaching an end. The original title by Fanon, in contrast, conveys greater caution and uncertainty, if not pessimism per se.[32] What is important to grasp is that, unlike *Black Skin, White Masks,* this book was written under conditions of acute political pressure, even if Fanon placed unwavering confidence in the Algerian people. In his 1965 introduction to *A Dying Colonialism,* Adolfo Gilly (1928–present), a Latin American activist, cites the tense atmosphere of the 1950s and 1960s: "Revolution is mankind's way of life today. This is the age of revolution; the 'age of indifference' is gone forever." Algeria had been "one of the great landmarks in this global battle" and Fanon one of its main chroniclers.[33] In Gilly's view, Fanon's writing is particularly notable for his depiction of the Algerian struggle's mass character: for presenting the conflict as not strictly military in scope, but ultimately holistic in nature. This populist quality presented the French with a challenge parallel to those the United States encountered in Vietnam and the apartheid government faced in South Africa.

Still, despite Gilly's sanguine retrospective assessment, *A Dying Colonialism* appeared at a difficult time. The book encompassed a crucial five-year period since the start of the war in 1954.[34] Though its publication coincided with the famous self-determination speech by de Gaulle on September 16, 1959, which signaled the likelihood of autonomy for Algeria, thus marking a key turning point in the war, it was still unclear if and how independence would be achieved, especially at the time of the book's writing.[35] In his preface, Fanon registers uncertainty: "Five years of struggle have brought no political change. The French authorities continue to proclaim Algeria to be French."[36] Yet, despite French military gains and the loss of momentum after the Battle of Algiers, change had occurred among Algerians, who demonstrated themselves as adaptive and autonomous through a range of idioms. In fact, the everyday "collective sufferings" documented in *A Dying Colonialism* directly inform the "national consciousness" that Fanon would elaborate in *The Wretched of the Earth*.[37] Nigel Gibson has characterized *A Dying Colonialism* as presenting "lived experience in terms of revolutionary transformation; [it marks] an attempt to communicate the construction of a new Algeria to a largely French audience."[38] It consequently serves as a crucial juncture between Fanon's esoteric first book and his final polemic.

*A Dying Colonialism* is a collection of largely self-contained thematic essays committed to addressing the hidden aspects of the Algerian Revolution—day-to-day sociocultural features underappreciated or marginalized within popular accounts of the war. Fanon dictated the book in Tunis, drawing from notes composed in Algeria.[39] Though designed to promote the FLN, its five chapters are more extended treatments of topic than the journalism he wrote for *El Moudjahid*. They build on the essay style found in *Black Skin, White Masks*. Moreover, the subjects of race, gender, and medicine explored in *A Dying Colonialism* highlight Fanon's own ongoing preoccupations, underscoring further continuities with its 1952 predecessor. However, suggestive of the influence of his intervening experience in political journalism, *A Dying Colonialism* is also more empirically focused and empathetic to a specific political cause. Fanon is less concerned with synthesizing his interests in psychiatry and philosophy to arrive at a unique critical position than he is with narrating and explaining the daily dimensions of the Algerian struggle. If *Black Skin, White Masks* posited a type of *psychological realism* for understanding colonialism and its effects on French citizen-subjects, *A Dying Colonialism* presents a *critical social realism* that stresses the physical circumstances of Algerian life. The former posed the fact of blackness against French claims of nonracialism; the latter posed the fact of colonialism (and anticolonialism) against views that would have Algeria merely be a part of France. The conflict directly influenced this turn from academic nuance, as the war demanded clarity and immediacy. Fanon called the Algerian Revolution "the most hallucinatory war that any people has ever waged to smash colonial aggression." His primary concern was to dispel this illusory psychological quality, to evince "the truth of the combat we were waging."[40]

In this regard, it is important to emphasize Fanon's commitment to present the conflict in human terms beyond the violence of the struggle—to outline the public and private aspects of Algerian existence during a time of total anticolonial war. These essays signal the complete respect Fanon held for the Algerian people and the conditions they endured. Furthermore, the combat being waged was not strictly by military means. Cultural resistance equally mattered. This intention contrasts with the many perceptions of Fanon as principally being an "apostle of violence" to achieve liberation—a view that Fanon himself challenged, since it undermined the humanity of those involved.[41] He notes in his preface that critics of the war "like to claim that the men who lead the Algerian Revolution are impelled by a thirst for blood."[42] *A Dying Colonialism* consequently presents a more sophisticated understanding of how Fanon comprehended violence, which rested in part on the distinction between the illegitimacy of violence as oppression (the French) versus the legitimacy of violence as resistance (the Algerians). The former was immoral, while the latter remained defensible.

But violence remained a fraught issue, as his introductory citation of torture illustrates. "In a war of liberation, the colonized people must win, but they must do so cleanly, without 'barbarity,'" Fanon writes. "The European nation that practices torture is a blighted nation, unfaithful to its history."[43] His purpose in comparison is readily apparent. "An underdeveloped people must *prove*, by its fighting power, its ability to set itself up as a nation, and by the purity of every one of its acts, that it is, even to the smallest detail, the most lucid, the most self-controlled people," he argues. "But this is all very difficult."[44] Fanon clearly believed in the legitimacy of the Algerian cause and the importance of demonstrating that, yet brutal acts of violence by the FLN represented this difficulty, an ineluctable fact to which he alludes. Because the revolution sought "a democratic and a renovated Algeria," the FLN condemned "with pain in our hearts" acts beyond its control, involving "those brothers who have flung themselves into revolutionary action with the almost physiological brutality that centuries of oppression give rise to and feed."[45]

Critics may accuse Fanon of being disingenuous, even actively misleading, in these passages by minimizing the FLN's culpability. Admirers may also think he is being too apologetic. He may also be implicitly critiquing the internecine strife within the FLN. Regardless, Fanon grappled with the issue of violence, and he spoke for the FLN. More importantly, his introductory remarks stage a larger purpose of the book. Fanon proposes that the Algerian War was not only about political independence. It also concerned the birth of a "new Algerian man."[46] "Colonialism is fighting to strengthen its domination and human and economic exploitation," he comments. "It is fighting also to maintain the identity of the image it has of the Algerian and the depreciated image that the Algerian had of himself."[47] The national struggle, in contrast, aimed to eradicate these images.

Indeed, the war provided a solution to the inferiority complex introduced by colonialism, as discussed in *Black*

*Skin, White Masks.* "The Algerian nation is no longer in a future heaven," Fanon declares. "It is no longer the product of hazy and phantasy-ridden imaginations."[48] The revolution had renewed "the symbols, the myths, the beliefs, [and] the emotional responsiveness of the people," thus establishing the fact, before the war's end, that "*colonialism has definitely lost out in Algeria, while the Algerians, come what may, have definitely won.*"[49] Fanon subsequently asserts that resistance is never completely defeated—or culminated. A distinction must exist between military actions and the deeper resilience of the human will. "What can it possibly mean, to vanquish a rebellion?" he asks. "An army can at any time reconquer the ground lost, but how can the inferiority complex, the fear and the despair of the past be reimplanted in the consciousness of the people?"[50] *A Dying Colonialism* ultimately documents this transformation in Algerian consciousness—its radical mutation, to reiterate Fanon—as well as the decline of a settler mentality.[51] In fact, his concerns did not rest with the Algerian people alone. They were also directed toward understanding "the man behind the colonizer."[52] In Fanon's words, "We want an Algeria open to all, in which every kind of genius may grow."[53]

These introductory remarks signal a departure from his pieces in *El Moudjahid* as cited, by engaging in more substantive argumentation over news analysis. The five chapters of *A Dying Colonialism* that follow outline further a sociocultural terrain that has continued to stimulate interest, including the importance of radio, the relationship between medicine and colonialism, and the predicament of Algeria's European community. Ato Sekyi-Otu has called these short studies "allegories of appropriation," due to their depictions of how Algerians adapted colonial knowledge, technology, and cultural practices for their own uses, concurrent with opposing foreign rule. Moreover, these essays, while self-contained in terms of topic, share a broad affinity by intrinsically resisting more conventional narratives of colonial dominance that left Algerians without agency. As with his first book, Fanon challenged once more oversimplified Manichean perspectives established by colonialism. He underscored instead the ways in which such distinctions were routinely dissolved and reinforced depending on the circumstances.

A key example of this critical approach is the book's first and best-known chapter, "Algeria Unveiled." Its title serves as a double entendre, referring to the veil (*haïk*) that Algerian women typically wore, as well as Fanon's aim of revealing the nature of French colonialism in Algeria. He specifically discusses how French officials concentrated on Algerian women as a focal point of colonial domination. They perceived allowing women to go without veils as a form of emancipation from traditional Islamic mores. But this colonial permissiveness had larger implications. "Converting the woman, winning her over to the foreign values, wrenching her free from her status," Fanon writes, "was at the same time achieving a real power over the [Algerian] man and attaining a practical, effective means of destructuring Algerian culture."[54]

Building on his critique of assimilation and the French civilizing mission in *Black Skin, White Masks,* Fanon thus positions the practice of veiling and unveiling as a microcosm of colonial control. For the Algerian woman, the veil is "the assertion of a distinct identity."[55] For the French official or settler, the veil reflected "religious, magical, fanatical behavior."[56] The veil equally underscored colonialism's sexual dimensions, returning again to previous themes. European men maintained an attitude of "romantic exoticism" toward Algerian women, with the veil literally and figuratively concealing their beauty. To unveil a woman accordingly expressed a form of gendered power.[57] "This woman who sees without being seen frustrates the colonizer," Fanon asserts. "There is no reciprocity. She does not yield herself, does not give herself, does not offer herself."[58] Colonial violence is one result, with the "rape of the Algerian woman in the dream of a European . . . always preceded by a rending of the veil."[59] Women nonetheless resisted Western acculturation. As Fanon describes, the veil posed "the organic impossibility of a culture to modify any one of its customs without at the same time re-evaluating its deepest values, its most stable models."[60] Counterassimilation as a strategy subsequently contributed to cultural and national aims.[61] Algerian women additionally became involved in the war through surveillance and political assassination.[62] In Fanon's words, the brutality of the French "demanded that new forms of combat be adopted."[63] The agency of women and the liberation of Algeria thus went hand in hand.[64]

This examination of tensions between local custom and colonial modernism continues in the remaining essays—to demonstrate not only how techniques of colonial control were subverted, but how they could be appropriated and revised for alternative purposes. Fanon discusses, for example, how Radio-Alger provided a means for the French to assert colonial dominance—a reprise of his earlier concern regarding the French language as an instrument of power. Algerians often resisted this technological intervention by simply refusing to listen.[65] Yet, during the war, the *Voice of Fighting Algeria* radio program provided a vital means for "consolidating and unifying the people."[66] Sociocultural changes are also observed. Fanon argues, spuriously in retrospect, that the Algerian family had experienced profound transformation facilitated by revolutionary conditions, with sons circumventing the traditionalism of their fathers, daughters enabling "the birth of a new woman," and, overall, the family "strengthened from this ordeal in which colonialism has resorted to every means to break the people's will."[67] Similarly, medicine, which had been "an integral part of colonization, of domination, [and] of exploitation," as cited earlier, had become part of the struggle, with Algerian doctors able "to supervise the people's health, to protect the lives of our women, of our children, [and] of our combatants."[68] These short studies—or scenarios, as in *Black Skin, White Masks*—therefore provide uncommon, firsthand insight into the war, presenting a unique lens on the domestic dimensions of the conflict, in addition to mapping the resilience of the Algerian people generally.

## Radical Entanglements—A 1950s Moment

The most intractable situation that Fanon addresses in *A Dying Colonialism* concerns Algeria's settler population, the subject of his final chapter. Indeed, this essay is the most significant, revealing the complexity of his politics and that of the FLN during the middle years of the Algerian Revolution. Titled "Algeria's European Minority," the chapter principally discusses the European awakening to Algerian nationalism, thus stepping beyond a predictable critique of settler colonialism. Fanon's argument is one of political inclusiveness in relation to French colons. It has often been neglected as a result—an inconvenient political stand vis-à-vis his popular image. Nevertheless, his stance reflected the position of the FLN's 1956 Soummam Declaration, which recognized the participation and role of Algeria's national minorities within the revolution—a political pragmatism that has typically been forgotten, and at times actively concealed, in the wake of a postcolonial state policy of Arabization that defined Algeria as Arab and Muslim.[69] The Soummam platform experienced debate and was eventually reversed in August 1957, before the December 1957 assassination of Abane Ramdane, who was its key theoretician.[70] However, *A Dying Colonialism* reflects the declaration's continued impact, at least on Fanon. Abane must be credited as a key influence on *A Dying Colonialism* and later *The Wretched of the Earth,* in the same way Césaire, Sartre, and others affected the conceptualization of *Black Skin, White Masks.*

In this chapter, Fanon points once again to the failure of the French Left to support the FLN, as he had in *El Moudjahid.* But, more significant, he cites the importance of white involvement within the liberation struggle.[71] "Another myth to be destroyed is that Algeria's settlers were unanimously opposed to the end of colonial domination," Fanon writes without hesitation.[72] He goes on to discuss Algeria's Jewish community, the political role of Europeans in urban areas, and includes lengthy verbatim testimony by two Algerians of European descent, who supported the FLN. "We know that many Europeans have been arrested and tortured for having sheltered and saved political or military leaders of the Revolution from the colonialist hounds," Fanon remarks at one point.[73] While this commentary can be construed as propaganda to garner further backing for the Algerian cause, it must be remembered that the 1950s comprised a fertile period of engaging with multiracial coalitions around the world— from the Bandung Conference, to the 1955 Congress of the People in South Africa, to the principles agreed to at Soummam. Fanon insists that the new society envisioned "*every individual living in Algeria is an Algerian*" and that, in a future sovereign state, "*it will be up to every Algerian to assume Algerian citizenship or to reject it in favor of another.*"[74]

This political accommodation contrasts once more with many views that perceive Fanon as a proponent of "Manichaean fanaticism," to use an expression of David Macey's.[75] But this inclusive politics, which stressed citizenship above all other identities, mirrored the demographic complexity of Algeria and the social entanglements that resulted.[76] It also justified Fanon's involvement in the Algerian struggle as a non-Muslim black man from Martinique. It prefigures his important distinction between national consciousness and more exclusionary forms of nationalism later addressed in *The Wretched of the Earth*. Indeed, these essays not only mark a maturation of style and argument from *Black Skin, White Masks,* but, as with his first book, they continue to challenge popular understandings that have Fanon consistently seeing the colonial world in stark terms. Many have underestimated the sophistication of his thinking. Similar to those of his contemporary Albert Memmi, Fanon's social observations possess far greater nuance than the topos of the colonizer and the colonized, with which he is typically associated.[77] While these political identities and sociocultural ontologies informed Fanon's interpretations, they did not overwhelm his worldview. Rather, he understood them to be fundamentally colonial in origin. Fanon remained committed to bringing clarity to the Algerian situation, but he knew that such lucidity required subtlety and gained strength through a precision fixed to actual social and political circumstances.

Despite its intention to reach a wide audience, *A Dying Colonialism* had difficulty finding a publisher, in contrast to his first book, and it was banned three months after it appeared—an unsurprising development, given that accounts from within the Algerian liberation struggle were rare and, as the French feared, could encourage support, a fact Fanon understood all too well.[78] Against these inauspicious beginnings, the book has left a lasting imprint, identifying thematic elements of the war that scholars have continued to pursue, in addition to advancing Fanon's own political and intellectual development.[79] His perspectives would continue to broaden over the next two years, as a result of new experiences in Ghana and Mali. His views would also depart from the FLN's ideological and strategic program, the latter of which became increasingly diplomatic in scope by 1960. Fanon, in contrast, would articulate a final case for grassroots revolutionary struggle, rather than political settlement, published just days before his death in 1961.

6

# *The Wretched of the Earth*

> For Europe, for ourselves, and for humanity,
> comrades, we must turn over a new leaf, we
> must work out new concepts, and try to set
> afoot a new man.
>
> —*The Wretched of the Earth*[1]

Frantz Fanon met Jean-Paul Sartre and Simone de Beauvoir for the first time in Rome in July 1961. He met Sartre
for the last time again in Rome in October, en route to
the United States for medical treatment. By December of
that year, Fanon would die of cancer.[2] De Beauvoir took
account of their first visit, writing that Fanon and Sartre
conversed for hours on meeting and ultimately spent
three days together. Sartre and de Beauvoir had left Paris
for Rome following a period of political pressure after
signing the *Manifeste des 121,* a manifesto containing
121 signatures by members of the French intelligentsia
who supported the Algerian struggle. As discussed earlier,
Fanon had caustically disparaged French intellectuals for
their ambivalence during the early years of the war, perhaps the most famous example being Albert Camus, who

sought an end to the conflict without a complete French withdrawal. Sartre and de Beauvoir's support therefore marked a significant turn, albeit a late one.[3]

Beyond this new political rapport and the fact that Sartre had deeply influenced Fanon's thought as seen in *Black Skin, White Masks*, de Beauvoir made a remarkable observation regarding their meeting—Fanon possessed a strong aversion to violence. This detail that emerged in conversation is perhaps unsurprising in retrospect, given its delicate treatment in *A Dying Colonialism*, in addition to his extensive medical experience in Blida and Tunis by that point and his consequent encounters with the physical and psychological effects of violence. Close friends and comrades of his had died—most notably Abane Ramdane, whose assassination in 1957 was attributed to fierce internal tensions within the FLN.[4] De Beauvoir noted that Fanon was also affected by the assassination of Patrice Lumumba (1925–1961), the first prime minister of the Congo, whom Fanon met at the All-African Peoples' Conference in Accra.[5] Still, de Beauvoir's comment decisively contrasts with the popular image of Fanon as an unapologetic promoter of violence to achieve political liberation—a perspective principally derived from his final book, *The Wretched of the Earth*.

Next to *Black Skin, White Masks*, this last work defined his intellectual stature, their shifting fortunes in popularity reflecting particular moods of political time and place. Unlike its predecessor, *The Wretched of the Earth* received an immediate enthusiastic reception—a fact that can be attributed to the relative fame Fanon had accrued by 1961, as well as to the auspicious timing of its appearance. Drawing its title from the Communist party anthem "The Internationale" ("Arise ye prisoners of starvation / Arise ye wretched of the earth"), it not only summarized and theoretically expanded on the Algerian Revolution that would end shortly, in 1962, but it also prefigured and rationalized armed struggles then emerging in Southeast Asia, southern Africa, and parts of Latin America. Furthermore, it would resonate with African American activists of the Black Panther Party (1966–82), who embraced a militant ethos in the wake of the assassinations of Malcolm X (1925–65) and Martin Luther King Jr. during the mid- to late 1960s. It presented a proactive alternative to the nonviolent resistance forged by King and others.

Indeed, it is important to observe that Fanon sought the broadest possible readership for this work, unlike *Black Skin, White Masks,* which was primarily directed toward an academic audience familiar with the fields of psychology and philosophy, and *A Dying Colonialism,* which principally targeted a sympathetic French and European audience that could provide support for the Algerian cause. If his first book stressed the importance of the unconscious, his last book, building upon his second, emphasized the urgency of conscious realities—a *political realism.* But the combative thrust that made *The Wretched of the Earth* an instant manifesto of Third World revolution has also rendered it more controversial—and its utility less clear in the present. Though the book made his reputation, it has been superseded in a number of ways by *Black Skin, White Masks* because of the latter's enduring contributions to understanding race and racism. The unqualified radicalism of violent struggle as a political strategy in *The Wretched of the Earth* has remained divisive in the decades since it first appeared. The anger the book possesses has not dissipated.

These qualities can partly be attributed to the well-known preface to *The Wretched of the Earth* by Sartre. Like "Black Orpheus," Sartre's opening essay risks overwhelming what Fanon subsequently argues. As David Macey has written, repeating an earlier assessment by Hannah Arendt, Sartre's preface is, "if anything, even more violent than Fanon's own text."[6] Alice Cherki has called it a betrayal.[7] Sartre himself commented that the book "had not the slightest need of a preface, all the less because it is not addressed to us."[8] Nevertheless, Fanon, already keenly aware of his mortal struggle with leukemia, actively sought Sartre's foreword for its intellectual validation, as well as for the promotional value it would grant the book in the public sphere.[9]

Sartre's preface in many ways continues the themes of "Black Orpheus" concerning voice and the culpability of Europe in acts of oppression. Western colonialism, he writes, had "Hellenized the Asians" and created "Greco-Roman blacks," echoing the title and content of his previous introduction.[10] "Its writers and poets took enormous pains to explain to us that our values poorly matched the reality of their lives," he further states, referencing Négritude, "and that they could neither quite reject them nor integrate them."[11] Yet Sartre was aware of the different world Fanon confronted. He had already prefaced other works that sought to capture the fraught politics of North Africa: Albert Memmi's *The Colonizer and the Colonized*, regarding the colonial situation in Tunisia, and Henri Alleg's memoir *The Question*, an account of torture by the French in Algeria, cited earlier. Indeed, Sartre presents *The Wretched of the Earth* as the articulation of a new political horizon—"the Third World finds *itself* and speaks to *itself* through his [Fanon's] voice"—even though the Third World was "not a homogeneous world," and its unity was "not yet achieved." It remained "a work in progress."[12]

The Third World depended on acts of creative resistance. Colonialism generated an explosive contradiction, by laying "claim to and denying the human condition at the same time."[13] "There is one duty to be done, one end to achieve: to thrust out colonialism by *every* means," Sartre writes. Fanon, in his view, demonstrates that "this irrepressible violence is neither sound and fury, nor the resurrection of savage instincts, nor even the effect of resentment: it is man recreating himself."[14] But Sartre also concludes on an important self-reflexive note. The political transformation Fanon articulates is not solely about the liberation of the colonized, "for we in Europe too are being decolonized: that is to say that the settler which is in every one of us is being savagely rooted out."[15]

*The Wretched of the Earth* must consequently be understood as providing *solutions* to the problems of racism and dehumanization that Fanon identified earlier in his career. Symmetry exists between his first and last books. Not only did the last pose a challenge to a European world order, but, like his first, it confronted those among the colonized who continued to consent to that order, with an approach less cerebral and more proactive than before, conforming to the realities of Algeria and the broader world it occupied.

## Situating *The Wretched of the Earth*

*The Wretched of the Earth* is Fanon's longest book and, though unforeseen as his final work until just weeks before his death, it summarized many of his long-standing political and intellectual ambitions. Composed in the elliptical discursive style found throughout his writing, it nonetheless achieves a stronger sense of political clarity, structural cohesiveness, and conceptual argumentation than the high-minded, eclectic, and often opaque *Black Skin, White Masks*. It is also more philosophically oriented than *A Dying Colonialism* by submitting a set of political theories, not just case studies, regarding decolonization. It is a work of political invocation, rather than criticism or social description as with his first and second books, respectively. These general qualities reflect a political maturation aimed at articulating a broad strategy and ideological coherence that represented Algerian aspirations, thus building upon his journalism and the influence of the Soummam Declaration, as outlined in *A Dying Colonialism*. Only two years separated his second and third books. Their composition overlapped. But distinctions must also be drawn, since the FLN itself continued to change, with Fanon holding an increasingly marginal position within the organization.

If *A Dying Colonialism* captured a certain party line stemming from the Soummam Conference, *The Wretched of the Earth* continued this approach by presenting a tacit internal criticism of the FLN and the GPRA's policies after 1958, perhaps even serving as an unspoken epitaph for his mentor, Abane Ramdane. Indeed, Abane is a more significant influence behind *The Wretched of the Earth* than Sartre, whose first volume of *Critique of Dialectical Reason* (1960), which cited the Algerian situation and the role of violence, also shaped Fanon's thinking.[16] Sartre must be decentered. Alice Cherki has written that Abane, "like Fanon, believed in the possibility of a new form of human interaction, a new society that could be achieved only through a revolutionary dismantling of the colonial state, and both men held out hope that Algerian Jews as well as Algerians of European descent would become part of the new Algerian nation."[17] Not only were they close "both personally and ideologically," but Abane's assassination indicated to Fanon the level of internal divisions within the FLN and "the erosion of the revolutionary mandate of the war of liberation."[18] Abane, who helped coordinate the Battle of Algiers in addition to conceptualizing the Soummam principles as mentioned before, had formed part of the FLN's hard line faction based inside the country.

In this sense, *The Wretched of the Earth* reasserted a set of revolutionary ideals concerned with the plight of common Algerians, apart from the exiled FLN leadership who, in contrast to the tactics espoused by Fanon, ultimately negotiated an end to the war. In fact, it is remarkable how infrequently Fanon cites the FLN by name. By then poised between an Algeria in talks for its independence and a sub-Saharan Africa still ripe for revolution, Fanon made a final appeal for the importance of popular struggle, as well as highlighting its dangers. The book remains an influential critique of Algerian nationalism, and nationalism generally, for this reason.

*The Wretched of the Earth* also continues Fanon's personal search for answers to questions raised in his first book—specifically, how to overcome conditions of inferiority and self-oppression that colonialism inflicted. It is perhaps self-evident that only decolonization, as theorized in *The Wretched of the Earth,* could provide a solution to the racism and alienation of colonialism, as analyzed in *Black Skin, White Masks.* But Fanon is quick to assert that political change alone could not diminish, let alone completely remove, colonialism's more lasting legacies. Decolonization only marked a political end point. It still remained a starting point for remaking humankind.

As with his first book, Fanon does not take a conventional approach, either through historical narration, tactical discussion, or organizational platforms. As with *A*

Figure 6.1 Frantz Fanon at the 1958 All-African Peoples' Conference in Accra. A motto of the meeting was "Down with Colonialism and Imperialism." *Permission granted and copyright owned by Fonds Frantz Fanon/IMEC.*

*Dying Colonialism*, he finished it quickly in a matter of months, aware of his declining health. However, its main positions experienced a long gestation. An initial appearance of his arguments, particularly for armed struggle, occurred at the inaugural meeting of the All-African Peoples' Conference in Accra in December 1958 (figure 6.1). A second conference was held in Tunis in 1960, with Fanon's involvement and with Algeria as the main theme, though the speech he delivered in 1958 generated a particular stir, given its critique of positions held by African leaders present, such as Tom Mboya (1930–1969) of Kenya and host Kwame Nkrumah, who advocated more diplomatic means.[19] However, the Accra conference did endorse the formation of an African Legion intended to promote armed struggle in Africa—an initiative that inspired Fanon's effort to start a southern front in the Algerian War from Mali, an ultimately quixotic plan formulated during his 1960 diplomatic stay in Ghana as ambassador for the GPRA.[20]

A second key moment in the development of *The Wretched of the Earth* was Fanon's speech at the Second Congress of Black Writers and Artists in Rome in 1959. Titled "The Reciprocal Foundation of National Culture and Liberation Struggles," this paper continued his earlier critique of Négritude—what he referred to, since the criticisms outlined in *Black Skin, White Masks,* as "the great black mirage"—by arguing for a national, rather than civilizational, basis for cultural resistance and autonomy.[21] Fanon did develop an affinity for the forward-looking, postcolonial pan-Africanism espoused by Nkrumah. But, like Nkrumah, Fanon cited the importance of nation-state independence first, in addition to the role of a broader Third Worldism for securing postcolonial sovereignty.

**On Violence**

Against this backdrop, Fanon's first chapter titled "Concerning Violence" resumes themes amplified in the preface by Sartre, though on terms specific to Fanon. It builds on his commentary on violence in *A Dying Colonialism,* and it remains one of his most influential and controversial essays. Several basic points should be made. First, despite enduring popular perceptions, Fanon does not advocate gratuitous violence or violence generally as a means of psychic catharsis. Rather, he proposes a defined set of historical origins and legitimate uses for violence. Second, pertaining to this first premise, Fanon depicts violence as a situated act, specific to colonization and decolonization. In his words, "decolonization is always a violent phenomenon," it "never takes place unnoticed, for it influences individuals and modifies them fundamentally."[22] Fanon's understanding of violence is directly drawn from the Algerian Revolution. Similar to *Black Skin, White Masks* and *A Dying Colonialism,* his discussion is socially grounded and based on his own experience. Third, Fanon locates the origin of violence in the foreign colonizer. "The colonial world is a world cut in two," with this division structured and maintained—spatially, socially, and politically—by the pervasive violence of settler colonialism. Only once the illegitimate violence that "ruled over the ordering of the colonial world" has been legitimately "claimed and taken over by the native" will revolution, at individual and societal levels, be possible.[23]

Anticolonial violence is, thus, in a Sartrean manner of speaking, antiviolence violence. This remark leads to a fourth point: armed struggle held the potential for personal transformation, by eradicating the ontological differences between colonial "settlers" and colonized "natives." These are the two central categories that Fanon employs from the Algerian situation and utilizes for his analysis.[24] These political identities notably depart from the specific racial terminology foregrounded in *Black Skin, White Masks*—a deliberate choice by Fanon that accounts for Algeria's demographic diversity, the complex political affiliations therein, and the ultimate importance of citizenship, as raised in *A Dying Colonialism*. Although they could carry racial meaning in practice, these political categories that colonialism introduced retained a flexible application, beyond Algeria, and a sense of impermanence, and thus were deeply tied to the political process at hand. "The destruction of the colonial world is no more and no less" than "the abolition of one zone, its burial in the depths of the earth or its expulsion from the country," Fanon writes, signaling the geopolitical and ontological dimensions of decolonization—or reconquest, it might be said—not sheer bloodlust.[25] Anticolonial violence, in short, provided a solution to the impasse between the colonizer and the colonized introduced in *Black Skin, White Masks*. This violence was not reactionary—an unconscious response to foreign oppression—nor reducible to planned military strategy. Faced with a choice between continued dehumanization or fighting against it, armed struggle represented instead a conscious step toward the eradication of colonial identities and the possibility of what Fanon called in his first book a new humanism.[26]

Fanon's engagement with violence—an unavoidable subject, given the character and longevity of the Algerian

Revolution—therefore marked an effort to reposition the issue apart from purely tactical considerations of the FLN/ALN's guerrilla struggle. Furthermore, it attempted to move the issue beyond the conflict's notoriety for viciousness on both sides, especially toward civilians. Fanon's support of anticolonial violence was set against the total violence—political, economic, and cultural—of colonialism. The intrinsic brutality of French colonialism prompted and shaped the ferocity of Algerian anticolonialism. This approach genuflected toward preceding philosophies that rationalized political violence, with Friedrich Engels (1820–1895), Georges Sorel (1847–1922), and Vladimir Lenin (1870–1924) among Fanon's precursors.[27] But contemporaries like Ho Chi Minh, Mao Tse-tung, and Fidel Castro equally advocated armed struggle as a political necessity.

Unlike these leaders, Fanon emphasized a transformative psychic liberation from feelings of inferiority instilled by colonialism. Fanon never picked up a gun in the same way these figures did. His views were specific to his training in psychiatry. Violence not only unified the colonized: it became "a cleansing force" that "makes him fearless and restores his self-respect."[28] It consequently provided a solution to the anxiety, the nervousness, the alienation, and the anger that Fanon diagnosed throughout his work. Sharing a professional affinity with Che Guevara, who similarly trained as a medical doctor, Fanon recognized the contradiction of being a physician and committed to armed struggle—a paradox never fully resolved, with the exception that his understanding and advocacy for decolonization did not conclude with violence alone. Violence was not an end in itself.

Dissolving the identities of settler and native—the pervasive political Manichaeism that obstructed social and political transformation—proved more important. Fanon describes at length the imbalance of power between these categories, how the "settler makes history" versus the native being in "a state of permanent tension."[29] Echoing positions in his first book, Fanon also reserves special criticism for the "native intellectual" who has assimilated to the culture of the colonizer and exists apart from the unity and will of the people.[30] "The native intellectual has clothed his aggressiveness in his barely veiled desire to assimilate himself to the colonial world," Fanon observes. "He has used his aggressiveness to serve his own individual interests."[31] By the same token, in a moment that can be seen as a critique against the position held by Camus circa 1956, Fanon argues that the Western "colonialist bourgeoisie" has invented nonviolence to supplicate the colonized and attain compromise, by insinuating a shared set of interests. Nonviolence is "an attempt to settle the colonial problem around a green baize table, before any regrettable act has been performed or irreparable gesture made, before any blood has been shed."[32]

This concern for the usurpation of political power by elites—whether a colonial bourgeoisie, native intellectuals, or nationalist party leaders—is based on Fanon's strong identification with the popular masses and their revolutionary potential, particularly the peasantry and the *lumpenproletariat* (landless peasants who have migrated to urban areas).[33] These social groups are, in titular fashion, the wretched of the earth. Their liberation—or emancipation, to invoke an older political tradition—is what Fanon sought. This terminology drew from Marxism, but with revision, given that Marx did not believe the peasantry or the lumpenproletariat could be a vanguard for revolution—a position more commonly espoused by Maoism. Fanon believed that Marxist analysis should be "stretched" when addressing the colonial situation.[34] Indeed, as Cherki writes, the "earth" in the book's title was quite literal, since it mattered greatly as a source of well-being and dignity to those whom Fanon represented.[35] Given that Algeria was predominantly rural, the 1956 Soummam Declaration had supported agrarian reform as part of its platform.[36] "The starving peasant, outside the class system, is the first among the exploited to discover that only violence pays," Fanon writes. "For him there is no compromise, no possible coming to terms; colonization and decolonization are simply a question of relative strength."[37]

But this inclination to violence must undergo a "ripening process"—it is not thoughtless or purely reactionary—starting from the time of colonial conquest. Moreover, it draws on "surrounding colonized peoples" and an "atmosphere of violence" emerging regionally and globally.[38] "A colonized people is not alone," Fanon offers. "In spite of all that colonialism can do, its frontiers remain open to new ideas and echoes from the world outside."[39]

160

This enveloping international atmosphere consisted not only of past victories, as with Dien Bien Phu, but recent events like the 1960 Sharpeville Massacre in South Africa and the broader, escalating tensions of the Cold War.[40] Colonialism persisted in different forms.

Despite the challenges of this geographic magnitude, Fanon's response to the global situation remained consistent. Paraphrasing a 1956 FLN tract, Fanon asserts that "colonialism is not a machine capable of thinking, a body endowed with reason. It is naked violence and only gives in when confronted with greater violence."[41] In fact, "the native chooses [a strategy that] has been furnished by the settler," Fanon concludes.[42] Still, beyond counterviolence were future challenges, including the need for the West to confront its responsibilities.[43] "Europe is literally the creation of the Third World," Fanon famously remarks in this chapter, referring to the vital role that colonies had in Western economic, cultural, and political development.[44] By the same token, he recognized the entanglement of the Third World and Europe. Decolonization would not necessarily result in complete autonomy. In an argument similar to his past assertions regarding the role of a white minority in a future Algeria, Fanon urges that a new world order requires a new humanism, one that would dissolve existing identities and political geographies entrenched by imperialism. In his concluding words to this chapter, Fanon demands that Europe not stand apart, absolving itself and avoiding responsibility, but instead assist the Third World, and with it "rehabilitate mankind, and make man victorious everywhere, once and for all."[45]

## On National Consciousness

Against this far-reaching backdrop that called for armed revolution, the next three chapters further deconstruct the political Manichaeism established by colonialism. This structure posed immediate strategic challenges as well as difficult, long-term legacies if not directly confronted. Indeed, these chapters are concerned less with the problem of *colonialism* than with the predicaments of *anticolonialism* and *postcolonialism*. In particular, Fanon positions "national consciousness" as presenting an ontology that could transcend colonial identities and their unconscious influence. Nationalism at the time, it must be remembered, was still *in medias res*. While not new, it remained an unstable concept and strategy. National liberation was not a predestined route. Integrating Marxist and nationalist thought together, as he did phenomenology and psychiatry in his earlier work, Fanon defines national consciousness as distinct from nationalism, the former being rooted in popular culture and history and therefore being broader and more inclusive than the forms of nationalism promoted by political parties and their elite leadership. This is a vital point. Nationalism was, and still is, often exclusionary on the basis of race, culture, class, gender, or region. Alternatively, national consciousness in Fanon's view tapped into local concerns and politics at the grassroots level. But it could only take shape if anticolonial movements actively worked against embedded differences that were structured by colonialism.[46] Fanon thus articulated a multipart critique of liberation movements, identifying locations of power and limitation both.

His second chapter, titled "Spontaneity: Its Strength and Weakness," is principally concerned with the precarious solidarities of struggle, due to these embedded differences among the colonized: between urban and rural activists, between party leadership and the masses.[47] Observing strains between common Algerians and an exiled FLN leadership, Fanon characterizes this relationship as distrustful—partly due to the intermediation of local leaders, but also to a perceived lack of organization among the peasantry.[48] This disjuncture could lead to political disregard, thus worsening relations, even after independence.[49] Reversing the location of political power, Fanon foregrounds the peasantry as the revolutionary vanguard with nationalist sentiment finding "an echo in the heart of the peasantry" where "memory of the [early] anti-colonial period is very much alive."[50] The lumpenproletariat further presented "one of the most spontaneous and the most radically revolutionary forces of a colonized people"—an urban base for the rural masses.[51] This argument for the role of a complex political consciousness among those most marginalized— the wretched, the damned—therefore extended points made in *A Dying Colonialism*. Fanon's remarks can be read as criticizing the exiled leadership of the FLN circa

1960, with its mounting neglect of conditions internal to Algeria. A divisive "interior" (inside Algeria) and "exterior" (outside Algeria) dynamic had come to characterize the war, with Fanon granting primacy to the former.[52]

Yet Fanon sounded a note of caution, acknowledging that rural leaders had been collaborators, as had members of the lumpenproletariat.[53] These facts threatened solidarity, as did the limits of revolutionary "spontaneity": its strength being its capacity to take form quickly, its weakness being its ephemeral nature. Persistence was needed; no battle was decisive.[54] Even racism, which provided an impulse for resistance, was not enough to "sustain a war of liberation."[55] "The native must realize that colonialism never gives anything away for nothing," Fanon writes. "Whatever the native may gain through political or armed struggle is not the result of the kindliness or good will of the settler; it simply shows that he cannot put off granting concessions any longer."[56]

But the longevity of struggle also enabled differences to break down. In a return to *Black Skin, White Masks,* Fanon discusses a persistent problem among the colonized: "The people who in the early days of the struggle had adopted the primitive Manichaeanism [*sic*] of the colonizer—Black versus White, Arab versus Infidel—realize en route that some blacks can be whiter than the whites, and that the prospect of a national flag or independence does not automatically result in certain segments of the population giving up their privileges and their interests."[57] Fanon thus reserved specific criticism for elites once more, whether colonial or postcolonial. Only struggle allowed for the circumvention of entrenched identities. "Many members of the mass of [French] colonialists reveal themselves to be much, much nearer to the national struggle than certain [Algerian] sons of the nation," Fanon observes. "The barriers of blood and race-prejudice are broken down on both sides."[58] Perceiving resolution to the predicaments introduced in his first book, he again concludes that the path beyond these forms of "mystification"—of colonial differences, by self-interested elites—is marked by violence: "Violence alone, perpetrated by the people, violence organized and guided by the leadership, provides the key for the masses to decipher social reality."[59]

But if violence presented a first step toward annihilating colonial ontologies, uncertainty remained as to what would replace them. For Fanon, national consciousness, not nationalism, provided an answer. National consciousness not only manifested a new political identity, it generated a status that transcended distinctions established by colonialism. Fanon acknowledged threats to this possibility, however, which inform his next two chapters. In "The Pitfalls of National Consciousness," Fanon advances an argument regarding political limitations, by examining how and why with "young and independent nations, the nation is passed over for the race, and the tribe is preferred to the state."[60] He continues to focus his attention on elites and their threat in undermining populist hopes. The appropriation of "the former European settlement" by taking over positions once held by Europeans, for example, reproduced a colonial structure of power that undermined broader prospects of political community like pan-Africanism.[61] "African unity, a vague term, but nevertheless one to which the men and women of Africa were passionately attached and whose operative function was to put incredible pressure on colonialism, reveals its true face and crumbles into regionalisms within the same national reality," Fanon contends. "Because it is obsessed with its immediate interests, because it cannot see further than the end of its nose, the national bourgeoisie proves incapable of achieving simple national unity and incapable of building the nation on a solid, constructive foundation."[62] This solipsism results in further social and political deterioration, with the bourgeoisie turning "its back more and more on the interior and on the real facts of its undeveloped country" to instead "look toward the former mother country and the foreign capitalists who count on its obliging compliance."[63]

The special vindictiveness toward liberation and postcolonial leaders in this chapter—a reprise of positions taken in *El Moudjahid*—was conceivably motivated by an increasing disillusionment with the FLN leadership as cited before, if not with its cause per se. Fanon does not directly outline such a view, but given his lower rank within the party, and the initiation of confidential negotiations between the French government and the GPRA in 1961, such an interpretation is plausible.[64] What is clear is that Fanon's arguments and the FLN leadership's own political maneuvering sharply contrasted. Indeed, the at-times opaque quality and abstract generalization found in *The Wretched of the Earth* can be understood as intentional, obliquely referring to the FLN without citing it by name. "During the struggle for liberation the leader awakened the people and promised them a forward march, heroic and unmitigated," Fanon summarizes at one point. "Today, he uses every means to put them to sleep, and three or four times a year asks them to remember the colonial period and to look back on the long way they have come since then."[65] Fanon promotes resisting this predicament, given that the bourgeoisie is "numerically, intellectually, and economically weak."[66] He cites gains in Algeria, where "we have realized that the masses are equal to the problems which confront them."[67] But, ultimately, the relationship between leaders and local communities—the building of national consciousness—must be mutually interactive, with "each citizen" contributing to a "period of national construction" and a "government which calls itself a national government" taking responsibility for "the totality of the nation."[68] Political effort must be holistic, driven by "an idea of man and of the future of humanity."[69] The "living expression of the nation" must reflect the "consciousness of the whole of the people" and embody a humanism that returned "dignity to all citizens."[70]

The roles of humanism and dignity—qualities that look beyond political decolonization—continue in his next chapter, "On National Culture," the essay originally delivered at the Congress of Black Writers and Artists in Rome. Though placed later in the book, this piece influenced his preceding arguments. Indeed, it forms a crux to his general position regarding decolonization as a process: if violence initiated such transformation, and internal societal and political divisions posed threats to its accomplishment, national culture provided a substrate for establishing national consciousness. It presented a basis for overcoming identities of race and political status once fixed by colonialism. In this regard, Fanon returns to earlier arguments by Aimé Césaire and others regarding the role of cultural politics, albeit with revision. Opening with an epigraph by Sékou Touré, the first president of independent Guinea, who insisted on fashioning "the revolution with the people," Fanon positions culture as "a special battlefield."[71] Colonialism's impact on culture was similar to that on the individual psyche. "Colonial domination, because it is total and tends to oversimplify, very soon manages to disrupt in spectacular fashion the cultural life of a conquered people," he argues.[72] Colonialism by "a kind of perverted logic" is "not simply content to impose its rule upon the present and the future of a dominated country," but "turns to the past of the oppressed people, and distorts, disfigures, and destroys it."[73]

National culture was essential in reversing this condition. It contributed to the process of overcoming an inferiority complex among the colonized. Fanon still criticizes alternative cultural efforts, including Négritude, for responding to such dominance by indulging a romantic past, instead of meeting the pragmatic demands of the present. However, he displays greater sympathy for such approaches than in *Black Skin, White Masks*. "I concede that whatever proof there is of a once mighty Songhai civilization does not change the fact that the Songhais today [in West Africa] are undernourished, illiterate, abandoned to the skies and water, with a blank mind and glazed eyes," he comments, echoing earlier criticisms. "But, as we have said on several occasions, this passionate quest for a national culture prior to the colonial era can be justified by the colonized intellectuals' shared interest in stepping back and taking a hard look at the Western culture in which they risk becoming ensnared."[74] Registering the importance of the precolonial past, Fanon admits that he too "decided to delve deeper," that colonized intellectuals "must have been overjoyed to discover that the past was not branded with shame, but dignity, glory, and sobriety."[75] "Reclaiming the past does not only rehabilitate or justify the promise of a national culture," Fanon further offers. "It triggers a change of fundamental importance in the colonized's psycho-affective equilibrium."[76]

Yet cultural politics must still be oriented toward the present and future. In his words, "the native intellectual who wishes to create an authentic work of art must realize that the truths of a nation are in the first place its realities. He must go on until he has found the seething pot out of which the learning of the future will emerge."[77] Art must have "pedagogical value."[78] It must constitute not only "an intellectual advance, but a political advance."[79] The past, properly utilized, should be employed with "the intention of opening the future, as an invitation to action and a basis for hope."[80]

Fanon concludes this chapter by underscoring the importance of struggle once more for establishing the conditions for a national culture to take hold. "The nation is not only a precondition for culture, its ebullition, its perpetual renewal and maturation. It is a necessity," he asserts. "First of all it is the struggle for nationhood that unlocks culture and opens the doors of creation. Later on it is the nation that will provide culture with the conditions and framework for expression. The nation satisfies all those indispensable requirements for culture which alone can give it credibility, validity, dynamism, and creativity."[81] This nation-focused argument decisively contrasts with the civilizational paradigm espoused by Négritude. But Fanon goes further. National culture must be produced *during*—not before, not after—the struggle. "The liberation struggle does not restore to national culture its former values and configurations," he remarks. "This struggle, which aims at a fundamental redistribution of relations between men, cannot leave intact either the form or substance of the people's culture. After the struggle is over, there is not only the demise of colonialism, but also the demise of the colonized."[82]

This is a key point. It underwrites Fanon's notion of a new humanism, which must be "written into the objectives and methods of the struggle."[83] Indeed, despite the same expression, this humanism is different from the new humanism introduced in *Black Skin, White Masks.* The latter formed an internal critique of Western humanism and its failure to achieve its ideals. In contrast, the new humanism of *The Wretched of the Earth* revises this earlier position to assert a broader definition made possible only through decolonization. This version is born and generated *through* national struggle. This argument revisits the claims of *A Dying Colonialism,* with its empirical case studies of a society undergoing fundamental transformation. Furthermore, in drawing a distinction between nationalism and national consciousness, Fanon believed that only the latter could lead to a more expansive sensibility. "National consciousness, which is not nationalism, is the only thing that will give us an international dimension," he firmly states.[84] Through a twofold process, national consciousness could instigate a concurrent international consciousness, as aspired to by pan-Africanism, yet one attuned to ongoing varieties of colonialism that rendered the postcolonial nation-state "fragile and in permanent danger."[85] Sketched only briefly, this global consciousness formed another part of Fanon's utopian ideal of a new humanism. It marked a commitment to broader political solidarities in the face of present and future threats to postcolonial sovereignty.

## On Trauma

Before reaching his conclusion, Fanon's penultimate chapter—titled "Colonial War and Mental Disorders"— returns to a technique found throughout his writing, especially in his first book: the medical diagnosis. Similar to its preceding uses, this clinical approach in *The Wretched of the Earth* grounds his rhetoric and arguments in first-hand observation. He resorts to his trained expertise to substantiate his assertions. What is striking about this chapter, however, is its contrast to his opening argument for violence. Indeed, it tempers his contentions regarding violence and liberation, thus further discrediting uninformed views that would have Fanon as an immoral apologist for violence. Fanon held no nostalgia for war, nor was he ambivalent about its effects. Through working with patients, he fully acknowledged the malignant pathologies that the Algerian War produced, with "disorders [that] last for months, wage a massive attack on the ego, and almost invariably leave behind a vulnerability virtually visible to the naked eye."[86] He presents four sets of cases—Series A, B, C, and D—drawn from his medical work from 1954 to 1959 that captured the trauma of total war, on Algerian and French sides alike.

Series A comprises five cases involving patients who experienced violence in immediate ways. These cases concern an Algerian man whose wife had been raped by French soldiers; an Algerian peasant who survived a massacre by French soldiers; an ALN soldier who killed a settler woman; and two European policemen who participated in torture, one of whom in turn was physically violent toward his family. These cases demonstrate both the psychic and physical ailments of violence—anxiety, insomnia, loss of appetite, hallucinations, and psychotic episodes of anger and violent behavior, among other symptoms. Series B involves psychiatric cases that were not reactions to the firsthand experience of combat, but reflect "the atmosphere of total war which reigns in Algeria": two Algerian boys (thirteen and fourteen years old) who killed a European boy; an Algerian man who suffered from paranoia; a young French woman whose father was killed; refugee children under the age of ten; and refugee women who had recently become mothers and suffered from depression.[87] Series C addresses victims of torture by physical assault, water, electricity, psychoactive medication ("truth serum"), and other techniques. Series D discusses psychosomatic disorders such as ulcers, insomnia, impotence, irregular menstrual cycles, and hypertension brought on by an environment of constant war.

These medical cases provide in acute detail the physical and psychic effects of violence for Algerians as well as French colons, in immediate ways and by living in surroundings defined and enclosed by violence. In this sense, the universal health effects of violence underscored the artifice of colonial identities, highlighting and eroding such distinctions at once. These cases reinforce the need to understand Fanon's fundamental aversion to violence once more, based on his intimate familiarity with it. The inclusion of this material should not be interpreted as undermining his initial argument. Rather, it stresses Fanon's own clarity and empathetic understanding about the stakes involved. He spoke with an authority from firsthand knowledge. In his words, such psychological and physical costs point to "the price of national independence" and, moreover, raise "the question of responsibility within the revolutionary framework."[88] He firmly assigns accountability to colonialism once more. In fact, Fanon revisits the stereotypic pathologies of the North African as prone to unthinking violence, to refute the physiological explanations and claims of primitivism by the Algiers school of psychiatry. "The criminality of the Algerian, his impulsiveness, the savagery of his murders are not, therefore, the consequence of how his nervous system is organized or specific character traits, but the direct result of the colonial situation," Fanon concludes. The war only intensified this psychological response.[89]

Violence was therefore not random, but the product of certain conditions. Or, as the critic Barbara Harlow has written, it is only random when history is disregarded.[90] Violence continues to be an important issue to debate vis-à-vis Fanon. Indeed, it must be debated, given the strong moral reasons and considerable successes of peaceful forms of political struggle and self-determination. But, in doing so, it is important to grasp the nuanced, even pragmatic, ways in which he understood it. Confronted with a decision between continued colonial dehumanization or actively resisting it, violence as an action taken remained a necessary cost for Fanon, if true and complete liberation, in all its dimensions, was to be achieved.

## A Literature of Combat

Departing from the clinical immediacy of his psychiatric case studies, Fanon's conclusion points once more to a broader political horizon, beyond Algeria. Its ambition is reminiscent of his final remarks in *Black Skin, White Masks,* though it is intellectually more confident and politically more hopeful.[91] In contrast to *A Dying Colonialism* and many of his pieces for *El Moudjahid, The Wretched of the Earth* confirms, not simply identifies, a new world coming into being through decolonization, if one still fraught with dangers. This world was not only postcolonial in scope but equally defined by Cold War uncertainties. "An end must be put to this cold war that gets us nowhere, the nuclear arms race must be stopped and the underdeveloped regions must receive generous investments and technical aid," Fanon comments early on.[92] But more pressing threats remained internal.

Fanon must be viewed as not only a critic of colonialism but a critic of postcolonialism. His skepticism of postcolonial elites originated from a range of sources— the political geography he maps extends from Africa, to Latin America, to Asia—yet it also drew from his diplomatic travels and his previous condemnation of African leaders. Their collaborative tendencies undermined the achievement and possibilities of sovereignty. "We may understand why keen-witted international observers have hardly taken seriously the great flights of oratory about African unity," Fanon remarks at one point, "for it is true that there are so many cracks in that unity visible to the naked eye that it is only reasonable to insist that all these contradictions ought to be resolved before the day of unity can come."[93] His criticism can also be understood

175

as registering disagreement with the GPRA, which had grown disconnected from the ALN's struggle inside Algeria. Fanon remained sympathetic to the latter faction, despite exile, through his ongoing medical work, as well as his diplomatic efforts in Accra and Mali.[94] As cited before, *The Wretched of the Earth* can be read as an epitaph for Abane Ramdane, whose vision of a secular, pluralist Algeria is one Fanon shared. The marginalization of such a vision within the FLN likely affected Fanon, even if his support of its cause never waned.

*The Wretched of the Earth* ultimately belongs to "a literature of combat," to use an expression of his. Similar to *A Dying Colonialism*, it was composed under extreme pressure within a context of war. More specifically, it was written to invoke and perpetuate revolutionary sentiment. It was not the product of idle thinking; Fanon did not have the luxury of time to refine ideas. A residue of incompletion inhabits this text. But unlike his second book, it displays greater certainty about the end of French colonial rule and what might unfold thereafter.[95] Like the work of Karl Marx, which analyzed capitalism in its infancy, Fanon's text is prognostic in scope, diagramming the essential elements of decolonization and postcolonialism in its infancy in order to cast light on the risks and opportunities for the future.[96] Indeed, *The Wretched of the Earth* possesses an anticipatory quality and tone—certainly of a new world ahead, but also, perhaps, reflecting acknowledgment of his own impending death. Finished while confronting this distinct likelihood, *The*

*Wretched of the Earth* inhabits a shadow space of political and personal twilight.

But this transition was greeted with energy, not resignation. If Fanon's politics were increasingly out of step with the FLN's by 1961, they gestured nonetheless toward countries further south that still held revolutionary potential. Fanon's final book endures precisely because of its total vision, one that disregarded political ceremony and stepped beyond conventional diplomatic approaches to decolonization. Fanon called upon "the whole people to fight for their existence as a nation . . . [to mold] the national consciousness, giving it form and contours and flinging open before it new and boundless horizons."[97] His book sought to expose the "naked truth of decolonization" and "the searing bullets and bloodstained knives which emanate from it."[98] "For if the last shall be first, this will only come to pass after a murderous and decisive struggle between the two protagonists," Fanon writes, without hesitation.[99] If *Black Skin, White Masks* possesses an intellectual restlessness, *The Wretched of the Earth* maintains a political impatience and unease. Both are hybrid texts that draw from multiple sources to extend the boundaries of the possible. Fanon stepped beyond his occupational limits as a psychiatrist in his first book. He transcended the roles of a diplomat and propagandist for the FLN in his final book.

*The Wretched of the Earth* ultimately raises questions about the definition and purpose of anticolonial thought—and the endpoints of decolonization. Though his book asserts a political realism by discussing the stakes of violence and the necessity of national consciousness, Fanon's concerns ventured far beyond aims of independence. He did not outline a theory of governance or statecraft. His broad conclusion, instead, regarded the birth of a "new man"—an incompletely defined notion that, nevertheless, he himself appeared to embody.[100] Furthermore, the Third World must "resolve the problems to which Europe has not been able to find the answers."[101] Imitating the West would only amount to "an obscene caricature."[102] Reinvention and self-discovery were essential.[103] The description *Third* had specific meaning—beyond First (the United States and Western Europe) and Second (the Soviet Union and Eastern Bloc) worlds, but also beyond the existing worlds of the colonizer and the colonized. The Third World constituted Fanon's civilizational paradigm. Decolonization in its total form offered far more than political independence. It promised the establishment of a new humanity, liberated from the constraints of Western imperialism and its political, intellectual, and ontological legacies.

# Transcending the Colonial Unconscious

*Radical Empathy as Politics*

> The density of History determines none of my
> acts. I am my own foundation.
> —*Black Skin, White Masks*[1]

The final journey of Frantz Fanon sent him to the United States, where he was admitted as a patient at the National Institutes of Health in Bethesda, Maryland, outside Washington, D.C. He had been diagnosed with leukemia in Tunis in early 1961, after a period of exhaustion following his return from the ill-fated Mali venture and a medical consultation in Accra. With few options, Fanon first received treatment in Moscow. But after limited improvement, he sought treatment in the United States, despite political misgivings. His hospital stay lasted for almost two months, from October 10 until his death on December 6, 1961. His wife, Josie, and his son, Olivier, accompanied him. Rumors have surrounded his death, specifically whether it was the result of malicious action.

The U.S. Central Intelligence Agency (CIA) was aware of his situation and, according to David Macey, was involved in arranging his stay.[2] But other, more immediate threats had already existed. The Organisation Armée Secrète (OAS)—a paramilitary organization founded by French military officers against Algerian independence, which had staged a coup in Algiers against de Gaulle in April 1961—had targeted Sartre and other signatories of the Manifesto of 121, as well as supporters of the liberation struggle more generally. Fanon had eluded a previous assassination attempt in Rome in 1959, possibly by the French or the Red Hand, an Algerian settler terrorist organization.[3] Factional differences within the FLN had also presented potential vulnerability, as in the case of his mentor Abane Ramdane.[4]

Regardless, Fanon was quite ill, and his medical prognosis was not an extended one. Indeed, such rumors surrounding his death contribute to an unneeded aura of conspiracy. But his passing at the age of thirty-six still contains several tragic ironies, among them his death in a country he cited as racist and neoimperialist and, more bitterly, its occurrence less than a year before the achievement of Algerian independence on July 5, 1962.[5] Perhaps the most significant paradox, however, is that independence was not attained in the end through the kind of cathartic violence Fanon promoted in *The Wretched of the Earth*, but resulted instead through political negotiation. Military maneuvers and forms of terrorism, especially by the OAS, continued. A political process, though, brought the war to its conclusion. A referendum held on January 8, 1961, had gained a majority of French support for Algerian independence, a turning point motivated further by the failed coup in April 1961. By March 1962, after months of secret diplomacy, a cease-fire agreement between the French government and the FLN was reached, with a second referendum in April approving the Évian Accords that established the terms of Algerian sovereignty. A third referendum held on July 1 for Algerians resulted in an overwhelming vote for independence. De Gaulle declared Algeria independent on July 3, with the FLN affirming independence on July 5.

This coordinated ending contrasts with Fanon's vision of liberation, though violence had clearly taken a toll. Given the timeline of these events vis-à-vis the publication of his last book in late 1961, Fanon was certainly aware that his hardline arguments departed from the political route then taking hold. His views remained grounded at a popular, rather than an elite, level, despite his service as a diplomat. Figures have been consistently difficult to confirm, but approximately 500,000 Algerians died (an FLN estimate) and over two million had been displaced, either by force (through detention camps, for example) or by fleeing into exile to Tunisia or Morocco—the latter figure reaching 250,000 total.[6] In contrast, roughly 25,000 French troops died, along with an estimated 55,000 pieds-noirs.[7] Roughly 800,000 Europeans left Algeria during its first year of independence.[8] From 1962 to 1968, between 140,000 and 450,000 Algerians, including many educated elites and French loyalists, also emigrated.[9] Perpetuating a cycle of violence, between 10,000 and 100,000 Harkis were killed out of vengeance, with fewer than one in ten receiving asylum in France.[10] Many continued to experience maltreatment and hid in Algeria, fearful of reprisal. Overall, as Martin Evans has argued, the Algerian War ultimately had a "diverse" violence that was fratricidal as well as oppositional, internal to Algeria as well as in metropolitan France. It was not reducible to a Manichean framework of Algerians versus French settlers.[11]

Amid these accumulated figures, the war had peaked by 1958 in terms of the number of Algerian participants and their combat activity.[12] Fanon's perspective on the revolution as found in *The Wretched of the Earth* is thus atypical, according to Matthew Connelly, a historian who has depicted the war as ending through a diplomatic revolution rather than a grassroots one.[13] This disjuncture between Algeria's negotiated (if also chaotic) transition to independence and Fanon's own political convictions poses fundamental questions of past and present meaning as a result. Though Fanon was not alone, since a hard line faction was well established within the FLN, this incongruity sounds a cautionary note about overrelying on Fanon and his views as an entry point for understanding the Algerian War.[14] An uncritical triumphalism must be resisted with regard to assessing Fanon vis-à-vis Algeria.

Indeed, it is essential to situate Fanon once more within a broader context to appreciate his arguments. By 1961, Fanon was poised between an Algerian situation reaching a diplomatic end and a sub-Saharan Africa still in the midst of decolonization and potential revolution. Figures like Léopold Senghor and Aimé Césaire had considered alternative federal models of self-determination, rather than complete independence from France. Fanon sought to define himself within this milieu and, as stated throughout his work, to speak to the present and future, however speculative that might have been. Unlike his intellectual predecessors, he witnessed violent revolution firsthand, as both a doctor and an activist. Such considerations explain how and why the purpose and resonance of Fanon's ideas extended well beyond the Algerian situation. Despite his persistent commitment to the Algerian people, the scope and substance of his intellectual ambition did not, in the end, depend on a specific outcome for a future Algeria. He stated his political beliefs without apology, unconcerned about his own party status or personal popularity. Measuring the meaning of Fanon's insights should not rest solely with the limitations, even failures, of the Algerian Revolution.

Algeria and France certainly changed in the wake of decolonization, a shift that not only further oriented Algeria toward Africa and the Third World but equally affected how France envisioned itself. In a number of ways, France became even more exclusively nationalist, sublimating the trauma of losing Algeria until the French National Assembly publicly recognized the war as a war in 1999. Historian Todd Shepard has argued that decolonization, in fact, enabled France to avoid addressing the troubling meanings of its imperial past.[15] Entrenching a sense of modern, civilized French-ness, the racism and religious discrimination of the French Empire have remained latent features of postcolonial France up to the present, thus eluding a call for fundamental transformation made by Fanon and Sartre in *The Wretched of the Earth.*[16]

Perhaps more damaging than these enduring legacies has been a postcolonial Algeria that has been unable to sustain its revolutionary ideals—including autonomy from France. Not only has Algeria remained divided along a religious and secular line—in part the result of a postcolonial constitution that stressed Algeria's Arab and Muslim character, a concern that Fanon had conjectured—but it has relied on French economic assistance and investment.[17] Eight years of war had left Algeria's economy in shambles. Compounding this situation was the flight of many from Algeria's educated class, leaving fewer skilled workers and business leaders to shape and guide Algerian development. Such factors of instability undermined the inaugural presidency of Ahmed Ben Bella, who cracked down on opponents and centralized power to secure his position. He was nevertheless deposed in a coup in 1965 by Houari Boumédiène.[18] Although Algeria remained a symbol of revolutionary Third Worldism during the Cold War, it faced internal and external challenges, with its political ideals compromised by the autocratic mismanagement of postcolonial elites.[19] In these ways, Fanon's arguments have remained prescient.

## Itineraries of Consequence

Fanon's life was quickly eulogized after his death. Friends and comrades recalled his political commitment and anger toward injustice, as well as his generosity and kindness to those around him.[20] Efforts were made by the FLN to return his body for an official burial in Algeria (figure C.1) as Fanon himself wished, though to the confusion of his family in Martinique.[21] A special 1962 issue of *Présence africaine* commemorated his life, with Césaire paying homage to his former pupil.[22] Alice Cherki describes how Fanon was celebrated during Ben Bella's brief presidency, with Frantz Fanon Day established to remember his contributions.[23] Only thirty years old, Josie remained in Algeria, becoming a citizen and working as a journalist.[24] She continued to nurture his memory until her death, by suicide, on July 13, 1989. Though Fanon's legacy would decline in Algeria during the intervening years, partly due to an official policy that effectively minimized his importance, Fanon's reputation nevertheless extended abroad, aided by translations of his work, its consequent discovery by new audiences involved in political struggles around the world, and, not least, the perpetuation of his life and work by his brother Joby and his children, Mireille and Olivier, in addition to Josie.[25]

As cited in the introduction, Huey Newton, a founder of the Black Panther Party, called Fanon a key influence on his militant civil rights politics in the United States—a perspective repeated by Black Power leader Stokely

185

Figure C.1 ALN soldiers carrying the body of Frantz Fanon across the border from Tunisia to Algeria for burial. *Permission granted and copyright owned by Fonds Frantz Fanon/IMEC.*

Carmichael (1941–1998).[26] But Fanon's more immediate impact remained on the African continent, where decolonization persisted as an issue. Amílcar Cabral—the revolutionary leader from Guinea-Bissau, whose influence extended to other parts of Portuguese Africa, namely Angola and Mozambique—shared a vision similar to Fanon's regarding the importance of armed resistance, the threat of neocolonialism, and the role of popular culture within national liberation struggles.[27] In South Africa, Steve Biko, perhaps Fanon's most important interpreter, drew extensively from *Black Skin, White Masks* for his own essays that sought to resist the psychological effects of apartheid racism and generate black self-empowerment in their place.[28] Lesser-known figures also embraced Fanon. Ruth First (1925–1982)—another antiapartheid activist, who was a member of the South African Communist Party and later assassinated in Maputo, Mozambique—extended Fanon's critique of postcolonial elites in her work *The Barrel of a Gun: Political Power in Africa and the Coup d'État* (1970).[29] Elsewhere, Ali Shari'ati (1933–1977)—an Iranian intellectual and activist—had corresponded with Fanon and later translated *The Wretched of the Earth* and *A Dying Colonialism* into Persian. Unlike Fanon, he believed in the revolutionary potential of religion, positioning him as a key thinker in the buildup to the 1979 Iranian Revolution.[30]

Since 1980, Fanon's influence has increased exponentially within academia. His work has provided a critical vocabulary that has been applied across disciplines, addressing such issues as the unending problem of racism to traumatic political violence like the 1994 Rwandan Genocide.[31] Yet, this intellectual range has also generated a distinction between Fanon and a secondary discourse about his work—what has commonly been referred to as Fanonism. This situation—a difference between his life and the life of his ideas—has generated debate, with scholars such Henry Louis Gates Jr. and Cedric Robinson both praising and deploring the appropriation and misappropriation of Fanon's insights. On the one hand, the use of Fanon has vitally underscored the pervasiveness of racism and colonialism in the making of the modern world. On the other hand, the frequent citation of Fanon has at times overwhelmed the discussion of these themes, to the exclusion of his contemporaries and other thinkers from different places and time periods—as well as to the exclusion of his own history.[32] Indeed, Fanon often appears to be everywhere and nowhere. He is unquestionably important. But it is equally important to situate him within a broader historical context, to place him within the specific strategies of the FLN, and to understand his diverse influences, whether Césaire or Abane, that informed his strengths and limitations as a thinker. By gratuitously referencing Fanon, we risk diminishing the potency of his insurgent thought and its specific intentions. He becomes a political cliché. A judicious balance must therefore be struck. As the postcolonial theorist David Scott has written, we should neither "rescue Fanon from himself nor . . . condemn him to history."[33]

This book has been written against this backdrop. It has sought to introduce Fanon, historicize him, and explain the reasons for his influence. By placing him within, rather than outside of, history, this biography has aimed to resolve the problem of selective memory and to demythologize aspects of his legacy, with violence and political Manichaeism being the principal subjects that have generated misunderstandings of his work. As discussed earlier, Fanon was not a one-dimensional advocate of violence. He condemned acts of violence committed by the French. And he equally condemned violence committed by Algerians whose actions worked against the aims of the revolution, namely the right to demonstrate the capacity to govern. "It is not easy to conduct, with a minimum of errors, the struggle of a people, sorely tried by a hundred and thirty years of domination, against an enemy as determined and as ferocious as French colonialism," Fanon writes in *A Dying Colonialism,* recognizing the delicacy of such matters.[34] Above all, he sought to articulate the demands that existed behind armed struggle. Indeed, though it is still morally imperative to debate Fanon on the question of violence, his critics tend to ignore this humane impulse behind his writing—his profound respect for the Algerian people—as well as the sheer pathological violence of French colonialism that not only oppressed Algerians but silenced their aims.

In similar fashion, Fanon did not uncritically promote either a racial Manichaeism in *Black Skin, White Masks* or a political Manichaeism in *The Wretched of the Earth.* In fact, quite the opposite: he positioned both as colonial formations, and swiftly sought to undermine them through various case studies as a result. These binaries *enabled* colonial chauvinism and violence by structuring ontologies of alleged difference. Asserting Fanon's continued relevance must take clear account of his nuanced views toward the colonial situation and of his seeming contradictions—deconstructing racism while acknowledging the social role of racial distinctions, supporting national liberation while cautioning against the effects of nationalism, promoting a new humanism while understanding the local meaning of cultural tradition, and believing in the importance of anticolonial violence while also practicing medicine.[35] Such tensions remind us that Fanon's arguments reflect a ceaseless search for solutions—driven by utopian ideals, yet grounded in political realities.

This sense of movement leads to a final point. Beyond anchoring Fanon's significance through his writing, as many have done, this book has argued for the importance of his life experience and how it informed and shaped his thought—the nonverbal, or actional, lessons of Fanon's legacy. Intellectual history, African and otherwise, too often privileges the written text. In the same way that his body of work challenges Western traditions of humanism, as Lewis Gordon argues, so too does his life expand the political geography of the Black Atlantic, by incorporating North Africa and a wider Third World—what is frequently referred to today as the Global South. Furthermore, while his politics are deeply tied to antiracism, class struggle, and resistance against forms of colonial and postcolonial oppression, Fanon reached these positions over time, given his background of relative privilege. His political arrival was the result of surpassing these origins by actively engaging with alternative geographies, social strata, and politics, which led to self-realization—his authentic self, one might say, in Sartre's definition.[36] Fanon consistently sought to transcend the racial, political, and intellectual ontologies imposed on him by colonialism. The middle-class son from Martinique became much more than his origins promised, through identification with surrogate paradigms of identity and experience, to articulate what can be called radical empathy.

As viewed through the lens of Fanon's biography, radical empathy can be provisionally defined as a politics of recognition and solidarity with communities beyond one's own immediate experience. It is a usable ethic drawn from his life. Disrupting more conventional politics of difference—whether on the basis of race, class, nation, gender, or culture, among other identities—it can be understood as an embodiment of the new humanism to which he aspired. It is also a strategy for achieving individual fruition through intersubjective engagement, to reference critic Hortense Spillers.[37] It is the result of a mutually constitutive process—a dialectic between self-knowledge and world experience—with geographic, cultural, and political mobility facilitating not only greater self-realization but the attainment of such awareness through commitment to causes beyond one's own background. Fanon's political, intellectual, and personal consummation did not occur in Martinique, but by living in France, Algeria, and Tunisia. Algeria in particular, as a place and situation, provided a means to think through predicaments, ideas, and solutions that had preoccupied him for much of his life. In this sense, it exemplifies what Édouard Glissant has called a "diversion" (*détour*)—an alternative means for finding answers, when local circumstances may not permit such discovery.[38] Algeria presented a different mirror. Committing a form of class suicide, to use Cabral's expression, Fanon placed his convictions in a struggle and a country that was not his own by birth. Yet his deep empathy for the Algerian people derived from firsthand experience through his role as a medical doctor, as well as his own sociopolitical (if not legal) status as a French colonial subject. Indeed, his critique of nationalism and his advocacy for secularism and pluralism are unsurprising, since they would enable him to claim a place in a postcolonial Algeria.[39]

Radical empathy as a practice consequently approximates Edward Said's notion of traveling theory and the politics that can emerge from itinerant epistemologies. In Said's view, Fanon's application of European thought to colonial situations highlights the uses and creativity that can occur under conditions of political duress. "To speak here only of borrowing and adaptation is not adequate," Said argues. "There is in particular an intellectual, and perhaps moral, community of a remarkable kind, *affiliation* in the deepest and most interesting sense of the word."[40] Radical empathy similarly resembles Nigel Gibson's understanding of Fanon's "radical mutation in consciousness"—the outcome of rejecting colonial Manichaeism and embracing the possibilities of political liberation as manifested through lived experience.[41] But perhaps above all, radical empathy as a political concept returns to a less-addressed theme in Fanon's work: the issue of love. As the scholar Nelson Maldonado-Torres has examined, the practice of love can actively subvert the politics of colonial difference, to create new spaces of autonomy and identification from below.[42] "True love, real love" is not being subject to others, Fanon argues, thus countering Sartre's influential definition. It is instead "wishing for others what one postulates for oneself."[43] As he writes at the end of *Black Skin, White Masks*, "Superiority? Inferiority? Why not simply try to touch the other, feel the other, discover each other?"[44]

Radical empathy as an ethic is therefore the precise opposite of those contrarian qualities often attributed to Fanon—namely, an unqualified support of violence and an entrenched Manichean worldview that affirmed difference. It is positioned against these lasting myths, with its commitment to alternative forms of identification and solidarity in order to transcend difference. Indeed, it elevates a complementary strategy against the dehumanization imposed by racism and colonialism. It breaks a colonial dialectic that has constructed enduring patterns of racial discrimination. As a personal action undertaken, it is the antithesis of the pejorative name-calling Fanon describes in *Black Skin, White Masks*, seeking to explode distinctions rather than reinforce them. Moreover, it does not displace or minimize his belief in the cathartic potential of violence—the brutal force of colonialism determining and shaping the brutal response of anticolonialism. Rather, it occupies the unspoken underside of this more vocal stance. Though this ethic clearly emerges in his second and third books, its most meaningful expression appears in actional, rather than written, ways through direct engagement with anticolonial struggle. Adolfo Gilly has written that Fanon was not interested in reporting the Algerian conflict in conventional fashion, but in determining its essence, especially the total capacity of Algerians "to make all the sacrifices and all the efforts, among which the greatest was not giving one's life in combat . . . but changing one's daily life, one's routines, prejudices, and immemorial customs insofar as these were a hindrance to the revolutionary struggle."[45] Fanon underwent this transformation himself. The element of complete participation is an essential aspect of this empathetic practice.

But this type of politics should not be applied to revolutionary conditions alone. Total liberation can occur only through the emancipation of all oppressed communities. The fight for human dignity was not and is not restricted to specific locales or social strata. Indeed, Fanon himself invoked this broader empathetic impulse through political comparison. Measuring Algeria against South Africa, he wrote that it was "a colonialism which is matched, on the continent, by its homologue in South Africa."[46] This comment echoes a similar comparison made by Nelson Mandela (1918–2013) in his autobiography *Long Walk to Freedom* (1994). Reflecting on his 1962 visit to the FLN/ALN base in Oujda, Morocco, just across the border from Algeria, Mandela remarked, "The situation in Algeria was the closest model to our own in that the rebels faced a large white settler community that ruled the indigenous majority."[47] Radical empathy was not limited to Fanon, but an essential gesture in the international politics of global decolonization.

## Silent Colonialism—Unfinished Projects, Necessary Futures

This concluding approach to understanding Fanon ultimately serves to mitigate the possibility of rendering him as an unreachable person through misguided mythology, whether positive or negative. It situates his contingent cosmopolitanism, redefines his political commitments, and opens a new set of possibilities as to how his legacy might be reconsidered and continued in the present. The practice of radical empathy is available to all, regardless of status, location, or time period. Through Fanon's example, it provides an alternative paradigm apart from race-based, nation-based, and similar solidarities of soil and descent, which can strengthen still existing colonial identities, as well as problematic liberal politics—namely, the so-called white savior complex, which persists in different forms—that reinforce, rather than emancipate, victimization narratives. Similarly, by emphasizing Fanon's genius, he becomes an isolated figure without tangible intellectual influences, a political martyr who did not possess human limitations, even failings. In the decades since his death, Fanon's thought has experienced wide interpretation, well past the social and historical conditions in which it took shape—a reflection of the capacity of his ideas, beyond the immediate circumstances of his life and the world he witnessed. But this treatment has also at times rendered his thought as too esoteric, as properly understood only on philosophical grounds or through abstract social theory, rather than on the basis of personal history and his persistent desire to communicate ideas through the prism of his own life, as his final prayer in *Black Skin, White Masks* submitted.

Fanon's writing is undoubtedly sophisticated, and he possessed distinct intellectual ambitions. He also sought to be understood—not by elites, but by common people. His writing accrued a more populist pragmatism over time, despite his resistance to relinquishing utopian ideals. Though Fanon is typically perceived as an independent thinker, he should equally be recognized as an intermediary—an interpreter of conditions and a purveyor of principles, both roles he embodied as a psychiatrist and as a diplomat. Poised between worlds and connected to different networks, his pursuit of self-knowledge and his refusal to be beholden to past legacies provide vital lessons for identity politics in our present and the exclusionary forms they can take. Fanon consistently worked against such pressures of history, such presumptions of personal origin, to attain a different set of possibilities for the future—to be his own foundation and, by extension, to aspire toward a new, more inclusive humanism unburdened by preceding hierarchies of racial, cultural, economic, and political discrimination.

This new, revolutionary humanism is still unfulfilled. Indeed, this book insists on the continued relevance of Fanon because his utopian project remains unfinished. Calling for sustained engagement with his ideas does not contradict his own declarations that his views be understood as fixed to a particular time and place. Rather, his arguments continue to be relevant because the conditions of racism, colonialism, and economic oppression that he fought against still exist around us, if in modified—and at times silent—form. Fanon belongs to a cohort of mid-twentieth-century Francophone intellectuals (such as Sartre, de Beauvoir, and Césaire), a generation of revolutionary activists (such as Mao, Guevara, and Lumumba), and a unique circle of thinkers from or shaped by Algeria (including Jacques Derrida, Pierre Bourdieu, and Louis Althusser). But he principally belongs to a black radical tradition, whose members have grappled with the need to preserve senses of heritage and identity, while at the same time aspiring to halt the dehumanizing effects of imposed racial difference. In the past, figures like W. E. B. Du Bois and C. L. R. James pursued these aims, while scholar-activists such as Angela Davis, Sylvia Wynter, and Paul Gilroy have wrestled with these periodically opposing intentions in the present.[48] Indeed, this tension between preservation and transcendence—what Fanon once referred to as "self-consciousness and renunciation"—has defined black critical thought during the twentieth and twenty-first centuries, as it has politics.[49]

In a manner akin to Fanon's desire to break from colonial ontologies of black and white, Nelson Mandela similarly looked ahead to a world without such distinctions, a point made clear in his court statement at the 1964 Rivonia Trial—better known as his "I Am Prepared to Die" speech—during which he argued in his concluding remarks, "I have fought against white domination, and I have fought against black domination. I have cherished the ideal of a democratic and free society in which all persons live together in harmony and with equal opportunities."[50] Such words are reminiscent of a passage in *The Wretched of the Earth* cited earlier, in which Fanon urges, "The liberation struggle does not restore to national culture its former values and configurations. This struggle, which aims at a fundamental redistribution of relations between men, cannot leave intact either the form or substance of the people's culture. *After the struggle is over, there is not only the demise of colonialism, but also the demise of the colonized.*"[51] The political imaginations of Mandela and Fanon were, thus, not only forward looking: they were total. Decolonization is not simply an endeavor political in scope. Rather, in its most meaningful expression, decolonization marks the annihilation of enduring colonial legacies, especially those in unconscious, hidden forms. It holds the potential to reshape the definition and course of humankind.[52]

This mutual recognition regarding the necessary transformation of both the oppressor and the oppressed on the part of both Mandela and Fanon—two figures, it must be reminded, who are typically contrasted on the basis of their views toward violence—indicates not only the pervasiveness of colonialism and racism in twentieth-century politics but equally the difficulty in overcoming such legacies. It is a project requiring not just the rejection of repressive political orders but the uncertain challenges of creating completely new ones. Both Fanon and Mandela understood that true political liberation—a revolutionary catharsis—demanded a completely new conception of humanity—one more expansive in definition and compassionate in purpose than had existed previously. Both, however, failed to see this achieved in Algeria or South Africa. Their political pragmatism that acknowledged the diverse societies they belonged to has been revealed to be too radical, too utopian, in practice.

But these ideals are not dated, nor out of reach. They remain urgent, ones that should be pursued without postponement. We still live in a world shaped and defined by a colonial past. Which is to say that anticolonial thought still matters. Transcending this inheritance requires the attainment of a humane compassion through a new political language, new forms of political solidarity, and, ultimately, the renewal of radical empathy as a political principle—an ethic Fanon and Mandela both cultivated, and exemplified.

# Notes

Note to Readers: The literature on Frantz Fanon, the Algerian War, the French Empire, and decolonization, among other topics in this book, is vast. Given the constraints of this series, I have cited only those sources I have used directly or those deemed essential.

**Preface**

1. Paulo Freire, *Pedagogy of the Oppressed,* trans. Myra Bergman Ramos (New York: Bloomsbury, 2000 [1968]), 54.

**Introduction. Unthinking Fanon: Worlds, Legacies, Politics**

1. Frantz Fanon, *Black Skin, White Masks,* trans. Charles Lam Markmann (New York: Grove Press, 1991 [1952]), 11.

2. Huey P. Newton, *Revolutionary Suicide* (New York: Penguin, 2009 [1973]), 116.

3. Edward W. Said, *Culture and Imperialism* (New York: Knopf, 1993), 60.

4. Patrick Ehlen, *Frantz Fanon: A Spiritual Biography* (New York: Crossroad, 2000), 13.

5. Henry Louis Gates Jr., "Critical Fanonism," *Critical Inquiry* 17, no. 3 (1991): 457–70. For related assessments, see Stuart Hall, "The After-Life of Frantz Fanon: Why Fanon? Why Now? Why *Black Skin, White Masks?*" in *The Fact of Blackness: Frantz Fanon and Visual Representation,* ed. Alan Read (Seattle, WA: Bay Press, 1996), 13–31; Cedric Robinson, "The Appropriation of Frantz Fanon," *Race & Class* 35, no. 1 (1993): 79–91; Immanuel Wallerstein, "Reading Fanon in the 21st Century," *New Left Review* 57 (2009): 117–25.

6. For recent appraisals, marking the fiftieth anniversary of his death, see Grant Farred, ed., *Fanon: The Imperative of the Now,* special issue of *South Atlantic Quarterly* 112, no. 1 (2013): 1–170; Lewis R. Gordon, George Ciccariello-Maher, and Nelson Maldonado-Torres, "Frantz Fanon, Fifty Years On: A Memorial Roundtable," *Radical Philosophy Review* 16, no. 1 (2013): 307–24.

7. Alice Cherki, *Frantz Fanon: A Portrait,* trans. Nadia Benabid (Ithaca, NY: Cornell University Press, 2006), 1, 2.

8. Achille Mbembe, "Metamorphic Thought: The *Works* of Frantz Fanon," *African Studies* 71, no. 1 (2012): 20, 26.

9. William B. Cohen, "The Algerian War, the French State and Official Memory," *Historical Reflections/Réflexions Historiques* 28, no. 2 (2002): 219.

10. Édouard Glissant, *Caribbean Discourse: Selected Essays,* trans. J. Michael Dash (Charlottesville: University Press of Virginia, 1989), 25.

11. Joby Fanon, *Frantz Fanon, My Brother: Doctor, Playwright, Revolutionary,* trans. Daniel Nethery (Lanham, MD: Lexington Books, 2014 [2004]), 109.

12. Albert Memmi, "The Impossible Life of Frantz Fanon," *Massachusetts Review* 14, no. 1 (1973): 9–39.

13. C. L. R. James, "Fanon and the Caribbean," *International Tribute to Frantz Fanon: Record of the Special Meeting of the United Nations Special Committee against* Apartheid, *3 November 1978* (New York: United Nations Centre against *Apartheid,* 1978), 46.

14. Frantz Fanon, "Blood Flows in the Antilles under French Domination," in Frantz Fanon, *Toward the African Revolution: Political Essays,* trans. Haakon Chevalier (New York: Grove, 1967 [1964]), 167–69. Alice Cherki claims Fanon did not author this essay. Cherki, *Frantz Fanon,* 107.

15. Mohamed Bedjaoui, "Frantz Fanon: He Took the Name of All the Oppressed," *International Tribute to Frantz Fanon,* 6.

16. Hannah Arendt, *On Violence* (London: Penguin, 2006 [1970]), 69; Elizabeth Frazer and Kimberly Hutchings, "On Politics and Violence: Arendt Contra Fanon," *Contemporary Political Theory* 7, no. 1 (2008): 90–108.

17. Josie Fanon, "His Solidarity Knew No National Boundaries," *International Tribute to Frantz Fanon,* 30, 31.

18. I am referring to a passage from Frantz Fanon, *Black Skin, White Masks,* trans. Richard Philcox (New York: Grove, 2008 [1952]), xviii.

19. Ibid., xvii.

## Chapter 1: Martinique

1. Frantz Fanon, *Black Skin, White Masks,* trans. Richard Philcox (New York: Grove Press, 2008 [1952]), 92.

2. I use Glissant's expression in a broad sense. Glissant was critical of Césaire, arguing for an Antillean epistemology of creolization against Négritude's Francophilic tendencies. See Maryse Condé, "The Stealers of Fire: The French-Speaking Writers of the Caribbean and Their Strategies of Liberation," *Journal of Black Studies* 35, no. 2 (2004): 154–64; Carine Mardorossian, "From Fanon to Glissant: A Martinican Genealogy," *Small Axe* 30 (2009): 12–24; Jean Bernabé, Patrick Chamoiseau, and Raphaël Confiant, *Éloge de la Créolité/In Praise of Creoleness,* trans. Mohamed Bouya Taleb-Khyar (Paris: Gallimard, 1993).

3. Orlando Patterson, *Slavery and Social Death: A Comparative Study* (Cambridge, MA: Harvard University Press, 1982).

4. Eric Williams, *Capitalism and Slavery* (Chapel Hill: University of North Carolina Press, 1994 [1944]). See also Joseph E. Inikori, *Africans and the Industrial Revolution in England: A Study in International Trade and Economic Development* (Cambridge: Cambridge University Press, 2002); Sidney W. Mintz, *Sweetness and Power: The Place of Sugar in Modern History* (New York: Penguin, 1986).

5. Vincent Brown, *The Reaper's Garden: Death and Power in the World of Atlantic Slavery* (Cambridge, MA: Harvard University Press, 2010).

6. John E. Drabinski, "Fanon's Two Memories," *South Atlantic Quarterly* 112, no. 1 (2013): 21.

7. C. L. R. James, *The Black Jacobins: Toussaint L'Ouverture and the San Domingo Revolution* (New York: Vintage, 1989 [1938]).

8. On this period, see Laurent Dubois, *Avengers of the New World: The Story of the Haitian Revolution* (Cambridge, MA: Harvard University Press, 2005); Sibylle Fischer, *Modernity Disavowed: Haiti and the Cultures of Slavery in the Age of Revolution* (Durham, NC: Duke University Press, 2004); Jeremy D. Popkin, *Facing Racial Revolution: Eyewitness Accounts of the Haitian Insurrection* (Chicago: University of Chicago Press, 2008). For the effects of Haiti on Martinique, see Rebecca Hartkopf Schloss, *Sweet Liberty: The Final Days of Slavery in Martinique* (Philadelphia: University of Pennsylvania Press, 2012), chapters 1 and 3; Gary Wilder, *Freedom Time: Negritude, Decolonization, and the Future of the World* (Durham, NC: Duke University Press, 2015), chapter 7.

9. Frantz Fanon, *Black Skin, White Masks,* trans. Charles Lam Markmann (New York: Grove Press, 1991 [1952]), 230.

10. Schloss, *Sweet Liberty,* 11.

11. Ibid., 2–4.

12. David Macey, *Frantz Fanon: A Biography* (New York: Picador, 2000), 48–51, 54–56. I qualify the issue of métis status, since Macey argues that Fanon's mother was illegitimate.

13. Ibid., 51–54.

14. Alice Cherki, *Frantz Fanon: A Portrait,* trans. Nadia Benabid (Ithaca, NY: Cornell University Press, 2006), 1.

15. Antonio Gramsci, *Selections from the Prison Notebooks*, ed. and trans. Quintin Hoare and Geoffrey Nowell Smith (New York: International Publishers, 1971), 3–4. Fanon's elusiveness with Sartre in 1961 is perhaps due to a sense of shame that a certain authenticity was missing: Fanon was not *of* "the wretched of the earth" per se, even though he identified and promoted their interests.

16. Joby Fanon, *Frantz Fanon, My Brother: Doctor, Playwright, Revolutionary,* trans. Daniel Nethery (Lanham, MD: Lexington Books, 2014 [2004]), 13.

17. Macey, *Frantz Fanon,* 54–60, 68–71.

18. On Césaire as a teacher, see ibid., 69. On Césaire's biographical details as cited, see Wilder, *Freedom Time*, 22; Gary Wilder, *The French Imperial Nation-State: Negritude and Colonial Humanism between the Two World Wars* (Chicago: University of Chicago Press, 2005), 151.

19. Robert Bernasconi, "The Assumption of Negritude: Aimé Césaire, Frantz Fanon, and the Vicious Circle of Racial Politics," *Parallax* 8, no. 2 (2002): 69–83.

20. Macey, *Frantz Fanon,* 67–71.

21. Brent Hayes Edwards, *The Practice of Diaspora: Literature, Translation, and the Rise of Black Internationalism* (Cambridge, MA: Harvard University Press, 2003), 17, 18. See also Edward O. Ako, "'L'Étudiant Noir' and the Myth of the Genesis of the Negritude Movement," *Research in African Literatures* 15, no. 3 (1984): 341–53.

22. Emily Musil Church, "In Search of Seven Sisters: A Biography of the Nardal Sisters of Martinique," *Callaloo* 36, no. 2 (2013): 375–90; T. Denean Sharpley-Whiting, *Negritude Women* (Minneapolis, MN: University of Minnesota Press, 2002).

23. Paul Gilroy, *The Black Atlantic: Modernity and Double-Consciousness* (Cambridge, MA: Harvard University Press, 1993). See also Imanuel Geiss, *The Pan-African Movement: A History of Pan-Africanism in America, Europe, and Africa* (Teaneck, NJ: Holmes & Meier, 1974); Colin Grant, *Negro with a Hat: The Rise and Fall of Marcus Garvey and His Dream of Mother Africa* (New York: Oxford University Press, 2008); Minkah Makalani, *In the Cause of Freedom: Radical Black Internationalism*

*from Harlem to London, 1917–1939* (Chapel Hill: University of North Carolina Press, 2011). On French Atlantic connections, see Christopher L. Miller, *The French Atlantic Triangle: Literature and Culture of the Slave Trade* (Durham, NC: Duke University Press, 2008). On Négritude's connections to Harlem, see Edwards, *The Practice of Diaspora*, chapter 3.

24. Abiola Irele, "Négritude—Literature and Ideology," *Journal of Modern African Studies* 3, no. 4 (1965): 499.

25. Abiola Irele, "*Négritude* or Black Cultural Nationalism," *Journal of Modern African Studies* 3, no. 3 (1965): 348.

26. Abiola Irele, "A Defense of Negritude," *Transition* 13 (1964): 11. Association had nineteenth-century roots, and both assimilation and association continued to coevolve up to the Second World War. See Raymond F. Betts, *Assimilation and Association in French Colonial Theory, 1890–1914* (New York: Columbia University Press, 1960); Frederick Cooper, *Citizenship between Empire and Nation: Remaking France and French Africa, 1945–1960* (Princeton, NJ: Princeton University Press, 2014), chapter 2.

27. Quoted in Macey, *Frantz Fanon,* 181.

28. Wilder, *The French Imperial Nation-State*, chapters 6, 7, and 8.

29. Aimé Césaire, *Notebook of a Return to the Native Land*, ed. Annette Smith, trans. Clayton Eshleman (Middletown, CT: Wesleyan University Press, 2001). For a critique of Négritude's radicalism, see Christopher L. Miller, *Nationalists and Nomads: Essays on Francophone African Literature and Culture* (Chicago: University of Chicago Press, 1998), chapter 1.

30. For debate on this issue, see François Manchuelle, "Le rôle des Antillais dans l'apparition du nationalisme culturel en Afrique noire francophone," *Cahiers d'Études Africaines* 32, no. 127 (1992): 375–408; Wilder, *Freedom Time*.

31. Jean-Paul Sartre, "Black Orpheus," *Massachusetts Review* 6, no. 1 (1964–65): 18.

32. Wilder, *The French Imperial Nation-State,* 260.

33. Wole Soyinka, *Myth, Literature and the African World* (Cambridge: Cambridge University Press, 1990 [1976]), 126–27, 135.

34. Michael Richardson, "Introduction," in *Refusal of the Shadow: Surrealism and the Caribbean,* ed. Michael Richardson, trans. Krzysztof Fijalkowski and Michael Richardson (London: Verso, 1996), 7. See also Suzanne Césaire, *The Great Camouflage: Writings of Dissent (1941–1945),* ed. Daniel Maximin, trans. Keith L. Walker (Middletown, CT: Wesleyan University Press, 2012).

35. André Breton, "A Great Black Poet: Aimé Césaire," in *Refusal of the Shadow,* 191–98.

36. Frantz Fanon, "West Indians and Africans," in *Toward the African Revolution: Political Essays,* trans. Haakon Chevalier (New York: Grove, 1967 [1964]), 26.

## Chapter 2: France

1. Frantz Fanon, *Black Skin, White Masks,* trans. Richard Philcox (New York: Grove Press, 2008 [1952]), 204.

2. David Macey, *Frantz Fanon: A Biography* (New York: Picador, 2000), 79.

3. Eric Jennings, *Vichy in the Tropics: Petain's National Revolution in Madagascar, Guadeloupe, and Indochina, 1940–44* (Stanford, CA: Stanford University Press, 2004), 9–10.

4. Macey, *Frantz Fanon,* 84–93.

5. Peter Geismar, *Fanon* (New York: Dial Press, 1971), 32.

6. Ibid., 36. Fanon mentions these episodes in *The Wretched of the Earth,* trans. Constance Farrington (New York: Grove Press, 1963), 307–8.

7. Geismar, *Fanon,* 35. Manville would become involved in the Algerian struggle, as a lawyer representing Algerian defendants. See Alice Cherki, *Frantz Fanon: A Portrait,* trans. Nadia Benabid (Ithaca, NY: Cornell University Press, 2006), 85.

8. Cherki, *Frantz Fanon,* 14.

9. Frantz Fanon, "West Indians and Africans," in Frantz Fanon, *Toward the African Revolution: Political Essays,* trans. Haakon Chevalier (New York: Grove, 1967 [1964]), 27.

10. Geismar, *Fanon,* 40–41.

11. There were breaks in Césaire's political career; see Gary Wilder, *Freedom Time: Negritude, Decolonization, and the Future of the World* (Durham, NC: Duke University Press, 2015), 109–10, 130.

12. Cherki, *Frantz Fanon,* 15.

13. On Martinique as a place of ambivalence, see Françoise Vergès, "Creole Skin, Black Mask: Fanon and Disavowal," *Critical Inquiry* 23, no. 3 (1997): 578–95.

14. Fanon, *Black Skin, White Masks,* 3. Senghor also served during the Second World War, though by then he had lived in France for over a decade.

15. Quoted in Cherki, *Frantz Fanon,* 15. Joby recalls this moment as an example of Fanon's humor: Joby Fanon, *Frantz Fanon, My Brother: Doctor, Playwright, Revolutionary,* trans. Daniel Nethery (Lanham, MD: Lexington Books, 2014 [2004]), 44.

16. Geismar, *Fanon,* 47.

17. Cherki, *Frantz Fanon,* 16.

18. Macey, *Frantz Fanon*, 26–28. Macey identifies the work of Homi Bhabha in particular. See Homi K. Bhabha, "Remembering Fanon: Self, Psyche and the Colonial Condition," introduction to Frantz Fanon, *Black Skin, White Masks*, trans. Charles Lam Markmann (London: Pluto Press, 2008 [1986]), xxi–xxxvii.

19. Cherki, *Frantz Fanon*, 16.

20. V. Y. Mudimbe, "Introduction," in *The Surreptitious Speech: Présence africaine and the Politics of Otherness, 1947–1987*, ed. V. Y. Mudimbe (Chicago: The University of Chicago Press, 1992), xvii.

21. Ibid., xviii.

22. Hegel's views were influenced by the Haitian Revolution. See Susan Buck-Morss, *Hegel, Haiti, and Universal History* (Pittsburgh: University of Pittsburgh Press, 2009).

23. Camus resisted being called an existentialist. See Robert Zaretsky, *Albert Camus: Elements of a Life* (Ithaca, NY: Cornell University Press, 2010), 96.

24. Jean-Paul Sartre, *Being and Nothingness: A Phenomenological Essay on Ontology*, trans. Hazel E. Barnes (New York: Washington Square Press, 1992), part one, chapter two.

25. Macey, *Frantz Fanon*, 133.

26. Cherki, *Frantz Fanon*, 18; Macey, *Frantz Fanon*, 138–39.

27. Macey, *Frantz Fanon*, 142.

28. Ibid., 145–52.

29. Cherki, *Frantz Fanon*, 21.

30. Ibid., 20. Macey claims Fanon's experience with Tosquelles lasted almost two years. See Macey, *Frantz Fanon*, 149–50. For further discussion, see Françoise Vergès, "To Cure and to Free: The Fanonian Project of 'Decolonized Psychiatry,'" in *Fanon: A Critical Reader*, ed. Lewis R. Gordon, T. Denean Sharpley-Whiting, and Renée T. White (Oxford: Blackwell, 1996), 85–99.

31. Cherki, *Frantz Fanon*, 81.

32. Ibid., 23. Regarding Fanon's return to Martinique, there is also disagreement. Cherki claims this visit happened in 1951, prior to Saint-Alban, whereas Macey says this visit happened after, in 1952. I have chosen the latter, since Cherki offers no clear evidence while Macey cites interviews with Edouard Fanon and Joby Fanon. Françoise Vergès has also confirmed the Macey chronology (personal communication, June 18, 2015). See Cherki, *Frantz Fanon*, 19–20; Macey, *Frantz Fanon*, 152–53.

33. Macey, *Frantz Fanon*, 154.

34. Jeanson would go on to support the FLN's clandestine activities in France during the Algerian War.

35. Quoted in Macey, *Frantz Fanon,* 159.

36. Cherki, *Frantz Fanon,* 25.

## Chapter 3: *Black Skin, White Masks*

Note: In this chapter, I have alternated between two translations of Fanon's *Black Skin, White Masks* published in 1991 and 2005. I have noted which edition I use for which quote.

1. Frantz Fanon, *Black Skin, White Masks,* trans. Charles Lam Markmann (New York: Grove Press, 1991 [1952]), 228.

2. Abdul R. JanMohamed, "The Economy of Manichean Allegory: The Function of Racial Difference in Colonialist Literature," *Critical Inquiry* 12, no. 1 (1985): 59–87; L. Adele Jinadu, *Fanon: In Search of the African Revolution* (London: Routledge, 1986); Benita Parry, "Problems in Current Theories of Colonial Discourse," *Oxford Literary Review* 9 (1987): 27–58; Patrick Taylor, *The Narrative of Liberation: Perspectives on Afro-Caribbean Literature, Popular Culture, and Politics* (Ithaca, NY: Cornell University Press, 1989).

3. On this period, see Frederick Cooper, *Citizenship between Empire and Nation: Remaking France and French Africa, 1945–1960* (Princeton, NJ: Princeton University Press, 2014), especially chapter 2; Gary Wilder, *Freedom Time: Negritude, Decolonization, and the Future of the World* (Durham, NC: Duke University Press, 2015). On earlier tensions between the ideals of French republicanism and the practices of imperialism, see Alice Conklin, *A Mission to Civilize: The Republican Idea of Empire in France and West Africa, 1895–1930* (Stanford, CA: Stanford University Press, 1997); Gary Wilder, *The French Imperial Nation-State: Negritude and Colonial Humanism between the Two World Wars* (Chicago: University of Chicago Press, 2005).

4. On blackness and France, inspired by Fanon, see Dominic Thomas, *Black France: Colonialism, Immigration, and Transnationalism* (Bloomington: Indiana University Press, 2006); Trica Danielle Keaton, T. Denean Sharpley-Whiting, and Tyler Stovall, eds., *Black France/ France Noire: The History and Politics of Blackness* (Durham, NC: Duke University Press, 2012). On the book's radicalism, see Christopher L. Miller, *Nationalists and Nomads: Essays on Francophone African Literature and Culture* (Chicago: University of Chicago Press, 1998), 41. On its failure to call for decolonization, compare with the explicit discussion found in the opening pages of Frantz Fanon, *The Wretched of the Earth,* trans. Richard Philcox (New York: Grove Press, 2004 [1961]). In the same way that James Baldwin was critical of the United States, but not anti-American, I believe Fanon, at this early point, was critical of France,

but not advocating decolonization. The intention of problematizing political thought in imperial contexts (i.e., the reduction of any form of resistance or critique as categorically "anticolonial") draws from Frederick Cooper, "Conflict and Connection: Rethinking Colonial African History," *American Historical Review* 99, no. 5 (1994): 1516–45; Christopher J. Lee, *Unreasonable Histories: Nativism, Multiracial Lives, and the Genealogical Imagination in British Africa* (Durham, NC: Duke University Press, 2014), chapters 6 and 7; Sherry B. Ortner, "Resistance and the Problem of Ethnographic Refusal," *Comparative Studies in Society and History* 37, no. 1 (1995): 173–93.

5. W. E. B. Du Bois, *The Souls of Black Folk* (Mineola, NY: Dover, 1994), 2. See also Stanley O. Gaines Jr., "Perspectives of Du Bois and Fanon on the Psychology of Oppression," in *Fanon: A Critical Reader*, ed. Lewis R. Gordon, T. Denean Sharpley-Whiting, and Renée T. White (Oxford: Blackwell, 1996), 24–34. On visibility, see David Theo Goldberg, "In/Visibility and Super/Vision: Fanon on Race, Veils, and Discourses of Resistance," also in *Fanon: A Critical Reader*, 179–200.

6. Homi K. Bhabha, *The Location of Culture* (London: Routledge, 1994), 61.

7. Fanon, *Black Skin, White Masks,* trans. Markmann, 7. Though published earlier in different forms, Césaire's book did not appear in its full version until 1955. See Robin D. G. Kelley, "Introduction: A Poetics of Anticolonialism," in Aimé Césaire, *Discourse on Colonialism*, trans. Joan Pinkham (New York: Monthly Review Press, 2000 [1955]), 7.

8. Fanon, *Black Skin, White Masks,* trans. Markmann, 7, 8. Césaire's true humanism is arguably more Eurocentric than Fanon's concept, but neither was thinking in terms of decolonization at this time. Rather, they were making an internal critique regarding the failures of Western humanism. Fanon would revise his position, discussed in chapter 6 of this book. See Césaire, *Discourse on Colonialism*, 73; Wilder, *Freedom Time*, chapter 5. On Biko, see Mark Sanders, *Complicities: The Intellectual and Apartheid* (Durham, NC: Duke University Press, 2002), 179–92.

9. Fanon, *Black Skin, White Masks,* trans. Markmann, 7.

10. Ibid., 12–14.

11. It should still be emphasized that the manuscript was composed over time and undoubtedly went through revision. See David Macey, *Frantz Fanon: A Biography* (New York: Picador, 2000), 134.

12. Frantz Fanon, *Black Skin, White Masks,* trans. Philcox, xvi.

13. Ibid.

14. Fanon, *Black Skin, White Masks,* trans. Markmann, 11.

15. Nelson Maldonado-Torres, "Frantz Fanon and C. L. R. James on

Intellectualism and Enlightened Rationality," *Caribbean Studies* 33, no. 2 (2005): 157–58; David Marriott, "Inventions of Existence: Sylvia Wynter, Frantz Fanon, Sociogeny, and 'the Damned,'" *CR: The New Centennial Review* 11, no. 3 (2011): 45–89.

16. Fanon, *Black Skin, White Masks,* trans. Markmann, 12.

17. Fanon, *Black Skin, White Masks,* trans. Philcox, 1.

18. Ibid., 21.

19. Ibid., 18.

20. Fanon, *Black Skin, White Masks,* trans. Markmann, 38. Ngũgĩ wa Thiong'o has made a related argument that European languages have damaged the African imagination. In contrast to Fanon, his concern is not that Africans have been unable to assimilate but that they have assimilated too much. See Ngũgĩ wa Thiong'o, *Decolonising the Mind: The Politics of Language in African Literature* (London: Heinemann, 1986).

21. Ato Sekyi-Otu, *Fanon's Dialectic of Experience* (Cambridge, MA: Harvard University Press, 1996), 26, 35.

22. Fanon, *Black Skin, White Masks,* trans. Philcox, 25.

23. David Marriott, "En Moi: Frantz Fanon and René Maran," in *Frantz Fanon's* Black Skin, White Masks: *New Interdisciplinary Essays,* ed. Max Silverman (Manchester: Manchester University Press, 2005), 152.

24. Fanon, *Black Skin, White Masks,* trans. Philcox, 29.

25. Ibid., 30.

26. Fanon, *Black Skin, White Masks,* trans. Markmann, 63.

27. For further discussion, see Amey Victoria Adkins, "Black/Feminist Futures: Reading Beauvoir in *Black Skin, White Masks,*" *South Atlantic Quarterly* 112, no. 4 (2013): 697–723.

28. Fanon, *Black Skin, White Masks,* trans. Philcox, xvii.

29. Fanon, *Black Skin, White Masks,* trans. Markmann, 84.

30. Ibid., 85.

31. Ibid.

32. Ibid., 93.

33. Ibid.

34. Ibid., 97, 100.

35. Ibid., 100.

36. Fanon, *Black Skin, White Masks,* trans. Philcox, 88. For a separate critique, see Césaire, *Discourse on Colonialism,* 60–62.

37. On these types, see Fanon, *Black Skin, White Masks,* trans. Philcox, 54, 57–62. On Fanon's innovations in psychiatry, see Hussein Abdilahi Bulhan, *Frantz Fanon and the Psychology of Oppression* (New York: Plenum Press, 1985). On interdisciplinarity, see Karen M. Gagne, "On

the Obsolescence of the Disciplines: Frantz Fanon and Sylvia Wynter Propose a New Mode of Being Human," *Human Architecture: Journal of the Sociology of Self-Knowledge* 5, no. 3 (2007): 251–63.

38. The 1967 translation still captures the fact of blackness in the face of French policies, as suggested at the start of this chapter, rather than a racial essence. On this new translation, see Richard Philcox, "On Retranslating Fanon, Retrieving a Lost Voice," in Fanon, *Black Skin, White Masks*, trans. Philcox, 241–51.

39. Fanon, *Black Skin, White Masks*, trans. Philcox, 89.

40. Ibid.

41. Ibid., 90.

42. Ibid., 95.

43. Ibid. Though Sartre's work on anti-Semitism proved a strong influence, Fanon insisted that Jews could "pass undetected" (95).

44. Ibid.

45. Paul Gilroy, *Against Race: Imagining Political Culture beyond the Color Line* (Cambridge, MA: Harvard University Press, 2000), 46.

46. Fanon, *Black Skin, White Masks*, trans. Philcox, 96.

47. Lewis R. Gordon, *Fanon and the Crisis of European Man: An Essay on Philosophy and the Human Sciences* (New York: Routledge, 1995), 6.

48. Fanon, *Black Skin, White Masks*, trans. Philcox, 102.

49. The general logic as articulated by Sartre is Hegelian in scope, with a thesis (white racism) countered by an antithesis (black antiracism) leading to a synthesis (the end of racism).

50. Fanon, *Black Skin, White Masks*, trans. Philcox, 112.

51. Ibid.

52. Ibid., 113.

53. Ibid.

54. Ibid., 113–14.

55. Ibid., 117.

56. Ibid., 114, 115.

57. Ibid., 132.

58. Ibid.

59. Ibid., 135.

60. Ibid., 138.

61. Ibid., 142.

62. Ibid., 169.

63. Ibid., 179.

64. Ibid., 178.

65. Ibid., 161.

66. Ibid., 124.

67. Karl Marx, *The Eighteenth Brumaire of Louis Bonaparte* (Moscow: Progress Publishers, 1972 [1852]), 10.

68. Karl Marx as quoted in Fanon, *Black Skin, White Masks,* trans. Philcox, 198.

69. Fanon, *Black Skin, White Masks,* trans. Philcox, 200, 201.

70. Ibid., 201.

71. Ibid., 202.

72. Ibid.

73. Ibid., 203.

74. Ibid.

75. Ibid., 202.

76. Ibid., 202, 203.

77. Kwame Anthony Appiah, "Foreword," in Fanon, *Black Skin, White Masks,* trans. Philcox, viii.

78. Ibid., 206.

79. Ibid.

80. Dennis McEnnerney, "Frantz Fanon, the Resistance, and the Emergence of Identity Politics," in *The Color of Liberty: Histories of Race in France,* ed. Sue Peabody and Tyler Stovall (Durham, NC: Duke University Press, 2003), 264–74.

**Chapter 4: Algeria**

1. Frantz Fanon, "Algeria Face to Face with the French Torturers," in Frantz Fanon, *Toward the African Revolution: Political Essays,* trans. Haakon Chevalier (New York: Grove, 1967 [1964]), 64.

2. Fanon, "The 'North African Syndrome,'" in *Toward the African Revolution,* 12.

3. Césaire argued that overseas colonialism led to continental fascism through a boomerang effect.

4. Martin Evans, *Algeria: France's Undeclared War* (New York: Oxford University Press, 2012), xii.

5. On citizenship in Algeria, see Todd Shepard, *The Invention of Decolonization: The Algerian War and the Remaking of France* (Ithaca, NY: Cornell University Press, 2008), chapter 1.

6. As quoted in Alistair Horne, *A Savage War of Peace: Algeria 1954–1962* (New York: The New York Review of Books, 2006 [1977]), 29. De Tocqueville also observed that the violence of French colonialism had worsened conditions. See the introduction to Alexis de Tocqueville, *Writings on Empire and Slavery,* ed. and trans. Jennifer Pitts (Baltimore, MD: Johns Hopkins University Press, 2001).

7. Evans, *Algeria,* xii.

8. On this period, see Benjamin C. Brower, *A Desert Named Peace: The Violence of France's Empire in the Algerian Sahara, 1844–1902* (New York: Columbia University Press, 2009); Jennifer E. Sessions, *By Sword and Plow: France and the Conquest of Algeria* (Ithaca, NY: Cornell University Press, 2011).

9. On this period, see James McDougall, *History and the Culture of Nationalism in Algeria* (Cambridge: Cambridge University Press, 2008); John Ruedy, *Modern Algeria: The Origins and Development of a Nation,* 2nd ed. (Bloomington: Indiana University Press, 2005), chapter 5.

10. Horne, *A Savage War of Peace,* 24.

11. Ibid., 26, 27.

12. Frantz Fanon, *The Wretched of the Earth,* trans. Constance Farrington (New York: Grove Press, 1963 [1961]), 78.

13. David Macey, *Frantz Fanon: A Biography* (New York: Picador, 2000), 244.

14. Ibid., 246.

15. Logevall cites both a figure for 325,000 Vietnamese killed (combatants and civilians combined) and a French figure of 500,000 Vietnamese killed (combatants and civilians combined). See Fredrik Logevall, *Embers of War: The Fall of an Empire and the Making of America's Vietnam* (New York: Random House, 2012), 619, 783n5.

16. Macey, *Frantz Fanon,* 245. See also Shepard, *The Invention of Decolonization,* chapter 2.

17. Fanon, *The Wretched of the Earth,* 90; Horne, *A Savage War of Peace,* 122.

18. Horne, *A Savage War of Peace,* 125. On Camus's support of Messali Hadj, see Olivier Todd, *Albert Camus: A Life,* trans. Benjamin Ivry (New York: Knopf, 1997), 61. See also Albert Camus, *Algerian Chronicles,* trans. Arthur Goldhammer (Cambridge, MA: Harvard University Press, 2013), chapters 21, 22, and 23; David Carroll, *Albert Camus the Algerian: Colonialism, Terrorism, Justice* (New York: Columbia University Press, 2008), chapter 5.

19. Other important figures at Soummam include Saad Dahlab (1918–2000), who helped found *El Moudjahid;* Benyoussef Ben Khedda (1920–2003), who later negotiated with France and briefly served as Algeria's head of state; and Krim Belkacem (1922–1970), who also negotiated the Évian Accords.

20. As quoted in Lou Turner, "Fanon and the FLN: Dialectics of Organization and the Algerian Revolution," in *Rethinking Fanon: The Continuing Dialogue,* ed. Nigel C. Gibson (Amherst, NY: Humanity

Books, 1999), 383. On the declaration, see also Evans, *Algeria,* 177–81; Irene L. Gendzier, *Frantz Fanon: A Critical Study* (New York: Pantheon, 1973), 175–76.

21. Alice Cherki, *Frantz Fanon: A Portrait,* trans. Nadia Benabid (Ithaca, NY: Cornell University Press, 2006), 104–6. On Abane and Fanon, see also Beläid Abane, "Frantz Fanon and Abane Ramdane: Brief Encounter in the Algerian Revolution," in *Living Fanon: Global Perspectives,* ed. Nigel C. Gibson (New York: Palgrave Macmillan, 2011), 27–44; Nigel C. Gibson, *Fanon: The Postcolonial Imagination* (London: Polity, 2003), 99.

22. Matthew Connelly, *A Diplomatic Revolution: Algeria's Fight for Independence and the Origins of the Post–Cold War Era* (New York: Oxford University Press, 2003), chapters 3 and 4.

23. On French troop numbers, see Evans, *Algeria,* 162, 275, 348. On FLN figures, see Horne, *A Savage War of Peace,* 321. Evans reports different figures of 20,000 guerrillas backed by 40,000 auxiliaries. See Evans, *Algeria,* 173.

24. Horne, *A Savage War of Peace,* 321.

25. On these numbers, see Evans, *Algeria,* 250. On the Harkis (the word *harki* in Arabic means "military movement"), see Vincent Crapanzano, *The Harkis: The Wound That Never Heals* (Chicago: University of Chicago Press, 2011).

26. Cherki, *Frantz Fanon,* 40.

27. Macey, *Frantz Fanon,* 212; Richard C. Keller, *Colonial Madness: Psychiatry in French North Africa* (Chicago: University of Chicago Press, 2007), 47-48.

28. Macey, *Frantz Fanon,* 215.

29. Cherki, *Frantz Fanon,* 60.

30. Keller, *Colonial Madness,* 48. Cherki cites a capacity for 800 patients, yet a number of 2,000 in 1953. Cherki, *Frantz Fanon,* 60.

31. Cherki, *Frantz Fanon,* 61; Jock McCulloch, *Colonial Psychiatry and the African Mind* (Cambridge: Cambridge University Press, 2006), 35.

32. On psychiatry and colonialism, see, for example, Matthew M. Heaton, *Black Skin, White Coats: Nigerian Psychiatrists, Decolonization, and the Globalization of Psychiatry* (Athens: Ohio University Press, 2013); Lynette A. Jackson, *Surfacing Up: Psychiatry and Social Order in Colonial Zimbabwe, 1908–1968* (Ithaca, NY: Cornell University Press, 2005); Megan Vaughan, *Curing Their Ills: Colonial Power and African Illness* (Stanford, CA: Stanford University Press, 1991), chapter 5.

33. Macey, *Frantz Fanon,* 214.

34. Richard C. Keller, "Pinel in the Maghreb: Liberation, Confinement,

and Psychiatric Reform in French North Africa," *Bulletin of the History of Medicine* 79, no. 3 (2005): 459–99.

35. For further discussion, see Keller, *Colonial Madness,* chapter 4.

36. Frantz Fanon, *A Dying Colonialism,* trans. Haakon Chevalier (New York: Grove Press, 1965 [1959]), 121.

37. Keller, *Colonial Madness,* chapters 2, 3, and 4; Macey, *Frantz Fanon,* 222–25.

38. Keller, *Colonial Madness,* 57.

39. Ibid., 17.

40. Cherki, *Frantz Fanon,* 62, 65.

41. Macey, *Frantz Fanon,* 227.

42. Quoted in Cherki, *Frantz Fanon,* 71, 72.

43. Ibid., 74.

44. Joby Fanon, *Frantz Fanon, My Brother: Doctor, Playwright, Revolutionary,* trans. Daniel Nethery (Lanham, MD: Lexington Books, 2014 [2004]), chapter 15. See also Macey, *Frantz Fanon,* 216.

45. Macey, *Frantz Fanon,* 242–43.

46. Cherki, *Frantz Fanon,* 63; Macey, *Frantz Fanon,* 259, 264-65.

47. Cherki, *Frantz Fanon,* 78, 79, 84; Macey, *Frantz Fanon,* 302.

48. Macey, *Frantz Fanon,* 296–98.

49. The exact timing and circumstances of his departure are murky. I have relied on Macey's account: Macey, *Frantz Fanon,* 299, 300.

50. Quoted in Macey, *Frantz Fanon,* 299. See also Fanon, "Letter to the Resident Minister (1956)," in *Toward the African Revolution,* 52–54.

**Chapter 5: Tunisia**

1. Frantz Fanon, *A Dying Colonialism,* trans. Haakon Chevalier (New York: Grove Press, 1965 [1959]), 28.

2. On his psychiatric work, see Alice Cherki, *Frantz Fanon: A Portrait,* trans. Nadia Benabid (Ithaca, NY: Cornell University Press, 2006), 112–14.

3. Frantz Fanon, "Racism and Culture," in Frantz Fanon, *Toward the African Revolution: Political Essays,* trans. Haakon Chevalier (New York: Grove, 1967 [1964]), 31–44. On its reception, see Cherki, *Frantz Fanon,* 88.

4. Cherki, *Frantz Fanon,* 101.

5. For a similar view, see Robert Bernasconi, "Eliminating the Cycle of Violence: The Place of *A Dying Colonialism* within Fanon's Revolutionary Thought," *Philosophia Africana* 4, no. 2 (2001): 17–25.

6. Ato Sekyi-Otu, *Fanon's Dialectic of Experience* (Cambridge, MA: Harvard University Press, 1996), 22.

7. David Macey, *Frantz Fanon: A Biography* (New York: Picador, 2000), 303.

8. Matthew Connelly, *A Diplomatic Revolution: Algeria's Fight for Independence and the Origins of the Post–Cold War Era* (New York: Oxford University Press, 2002), 74.

9. Cherki, *Frantz Fanon,* 102.

10. Ibid., 102–4. Josie also found employment as a journalist.

11. Macey, *Frantz Fanon,* 331.

12. Ibid., 329.

13. Fanon, *A Dying Colonialism,* chapter 2.

14. Cherki, *Frantz Fanon,* 107.

15. Pieces by Fanon are also missing in *Toward the African Revolution.* See ibid.

16. Fanon, "Disappointments and Illusions of French Colonialism," in *Toward the African Revolution,* 57–63; Fanon, "Algeria Face to Face with the French Torturers," in *Toward the African Revolution,* 64–72.

17. Fanon, "Algeria Face to Face with the French Torturers," 66.

18. Cherki, *Frantz Fanon,* 95; Macey, *Frantz Fanon,* 248, 341.

19. Cherki, *Frantz Fanon,* 95.

20. James Le Sueur, *Uncivil War: Intellectuals and Identity Politics during the Decolonization of Algeria,* 2nd ed. (Lincoln: University of Nebraska Press, 2005), 207–10, 210.

21. Fanon, "Maghreb Blood Shall Not Flow in Vain," in *Toward the African Revolution,* 91–95; Fanon, "Decolonization and Independence," in *Toward the African Revolution,* 99–105.

22. Connelly, *A Diplomatic Revolution,* 194–95. On Fanon's passport, see Macey, *Frantz Fanon,* 358. On Fanon's 1959 visit to Oudja, see Macey, *Frantz Fanon,* 392–93.

23. On the Fourth Republic and de Gaulle, see Todd Shepard, *The Invention of Decolonization: The Algerian War and the Remaking of France* (Ithaca, NY: Cornell University Press, 2008), part I.

24. The People's Republic of China was also seeking international recognition and legitimacy at the time, following its communist revolution. On Bandung, see Connelly, *A Diplomatic Revolution,* 9, 81; Alistair Horne, *A Savage War of Peace: Algeria 1954–1962* (New York: The New York Review of Books, 2006), 130–31.

25. Fanon, "A Continued Crisis," in *Toward the African Revolution,* 109.

26. Ibid., 108.

27. Fanon, "Letter to the Youth of Africa," in *Toward the African Revolution,* 117.

28. Fanon, "First Truths on the Colonial Problem," in *Toward the African Revolution*, 121.

29. Fanon, "The Algerian War and Man's Liberation," in *Toward the African Revolution*, 145. On Guinea, see Elizabeth Schmidt, *Cold War and Decolonization in Guinea, 1946–1958* (Athens: Ohio University Press, 2007).

30. Fanon, "The Algerian War and Man's Liberation," 146.

31. Fanon, "Algeria in Accra," in *Toward the African Revolution,* 150–52; Fanon, "Accra: Africa Affirms Its Unity and Defines Its Strategy," in *Toward the African Revolution,* 153–57.

32. Fanon originally wanted to entitle it *Réalité d'une nation*, and a 1966 second edition had the title *Sociologie de la Révolution algérienne.* Macey argues that the English title obscures an important reference, namely, "'Year V' alludes to the revolutionary calendar that made 1789 'Year I of the French Revolution' and expresses Fanon's conviction that a new historical era had begun on 1 November 1954." Macey, *Frantz Fanon,* 398.

33. Adolfo Gilly, "Introduction," in Fanon, *A Dying Colonialism*, 1, 2.

34. Ibid., 9.

35. Fanon's preface is dated July 1959. See Fanon, *A Dying Colonialism,* 33. On de Gaulle's speech, see Martin Evans, *Algeria: France's Undeclared War* (New York: Oxford University Press, 2012), chapter 9.

36. Fanon, *A Dying Colonialism,* 23.

37. Ibid., 28.

38. Nigel C. Gibson, *Fanon: The Postcolonial Imagination* (Cambridge: Polity, 2003), 4.

39. Cherki, *Frantz Fanon,* 116.

40. Fanon, *A Dying Colonialism,* 23.

41. Emmanuel Hansen, "Frantz Fanon: Portrait of a Revolutionary," in *Rethinking Fanon: The Continuing Dialogue,* ed. Nigel C. Gibson (Amherst, NY: Humanity Books, 1999), 81.

42. Fanon, *A Dying Colonialism,* 23.

43. Ibid., 24.

44. My emphasis. Ibid.

45. Ibid., 25.

46. Ibid., 30.

47. Ibid.

48. Ibid.

49. Ibid., 30, 31.

50. Ibid., 31.

51. Ibid., 32.

52. Ibid.

53. Ibid.

54. Ibid., 39.

55. Ibid., 41.

56. Ibid.

57. Ibid., 43.

58. Ibid., 44.

59. Ibid., 45.

60. Ibid., 41–42.

61. Ibid., 42.

62. Ibid., 48, 53, 57.

63. Ibid., 57.

64. Fanon has experienced criticism for factual errors regarding the involvement of Algerian women, for reproducing Eurocentric views, and for reinforcing patriarchal norms. See Drucilla Cornell, "The Secret Behind the Veil: A Reinterpretation of 'Algeria Unveiled,'" *Philosophia Africana* 4, no. 2 (2001): 27–35; Marie-Aimée Helie-Lucas, "Women, Nationalism, and Religion in the Algerian Liberation Struggle," in *Rethinking Fanon,* 271–82; Anne McClintock, "Fanon and Gender Agency," in *Rethinking Fanon,* 288–93; T. Denean Sharpley-Whiting, *Frantz Fanon: Conflicts and Feminisms* (Lanham, MD: Rowman & Littlefield, 1997).

65. Fanon, *A Dying Colonialism,* 72, 73.

66. Ibid., 84.

67. Ibid., 103–5, 107, 116.

68. Ibid., 134, 142.

69. Cherki, *Frantz Fanon,* 105–6; Irene L. Gendzier, *Frantz Fanon: A Critical Study* (New York: Pantheon, 1973), 175–81; Gibson, *Fanon,* 99; Charles F. Peterson, *Du Bois, Fanon, Cabral: The Margins of Elite Anti-Colonial Leadership* (Lanham, MD: Lexington Books, 2007), 97–99.

70. Evans, *Algeria,* 228.

71. Fanon, *A Dying Colonialism,* 147, 150–51.

72. Ibid., 157.

73. Ibid., 162.

74. Ibid., 152.

75. Macey, *Frantz Fanon,* 401.

76. Beläid Abane, "Frantz Fanon and Abane Ramdane: Brief Encounter in the Algerian Revolution," in *Living Fanon: Global Perspectives,* ed. Nigel C. Gibson (New York: Palgrave Macmillan, 2011), 39. Abane himself was a member of the Berber cultural minority of the Kabylia region.

77. Memmi takes care in defining his terms; see Albert Memmi, *The*

*Colonizer and the Colonized,* trans. Howard Greenfeld (Boston: Beacon Press, 1991 [1957]), 10, 11, 120.

78. Macey, *Frantz Fanon,* 410.

79. For a different source on this period, see Mouloud Feraoun, *Journal, 1955–1962: Reflections on the French-Algerian War,* trans. Mary Ellen Wolf and Claude Fouillade (Lincoln, NE: Bison Books, 2000 [1962]).

### Chapter 6: *The Wretched of the Earth*

Note: I have alternated between two translations of *The Wretched of the Earth,* noting which edition I use for which quotation.

1. Frantz Fanon, *The Wretched of the Earth,* trans. Constance Farrington (New York: Grove Press, 1963 [1961]), 316.

2. Alice Cherki, *Frantz Fanon: A Portrait,* trans. Nadia Benabid (Ithaca, NY: Cornell University Press, 2006), 164–65.

3. Camus, Sartre, and de Beauvoir had a tense relationship. For an overview of this scene, see James Le Sueur, *Uncivil War: Intellectuals and Identity Politics during the Decolonization of Algeria* (Philadelphia: University of Pennsylvania Press, 2001).

4. On Abane's death, see Cherki, *Frantz Fanon,* 105; Martin Evans, *Algeria: France's Undeclared War* (New York: Oxford University Press, 2012), 226; David Macey, *Frantz Fanon: A Biography* (New York: Picador, 2000), 356–57. On internal tensions within the FLN, including those between Ahmed Ben Bella and Abane, see Evans, *Algeria,* 129, 179, 228–29; Macey, *Frantz Fanon,* 306, 338. Ethnic identities also explain tensions between Arab and Berber factions, though such differences must be treated with caution, since the French had exploited such distinctions as a matter of divide-and-rule. See Evans, *Algeria,* 10, 60, 108–9, 357.

5. Macey, *Frantz Fanon,* 356–57.

6. Hannah Arendt, *On Violence* (New York: Harcourt, 1970), 12; Macey, *Frantz Fanon,* 464.

7. Cherki, *Frantz Fanon,* 181.

8. Jean-Paul Sartre, "Preface," in Frantz Fanon, *The Wretched of the Earth,* trans. Constance Farrington (New York: Grove Press, 1963 [1961]), 24.

9. Cherki, *Frantz Fanon,* 162–63.

10. Jean-Paul Sartre, "Preface," in Frantz Fanon, *The Wretched of the Earth,* trans. Richard Philcox (New York: Grove Press, 2004 [1961]), xliv.

11. Ibid.

12. Sartre, "Preface," in *The Wretched of the Earth,* trans. Farrington, 10, 11.

13. Ibid., 20.

14. Ibid., 21.

15. Ibid., 24. For further discussion, see Judith Butler, "Violence, Non-Violence: Sartre on Fanon," *Graduate Faculty Philosophy Journal* 27, no. 1 (2006): 3–24.

16. Beläid Abane, "Frantz Fanon and Abane Ramdane: Brief Encounter in the Algerian Revolution," in *Living Fanon: Global Perspectives,* ed. Nigel C. Gibson (New York: Palgrave Macmillan, 2011), 27, 28; Gerard Aching, "No Need for an Apology: Fanon's Untimely Critique of Political Consciousness," *South Atlantic Quarterly* 112, no. 1 (2013): 30; Cherki, *Frantz Fanon,* 160; Nigel C. Gibson, *Fanon: The Postcolonial Imagination* (London: Polity, 2003), 99; Macey, *Frantz Fanon,* 460. Albert Camus and Simone de Beauvoir addressed violence, though their impact on Fanon is less clear. See Albert Camus, *The Rebel: An Essay on Man in Revolt,* trans. Anthony Bower (New York: Vintage, 1992 [1951]); Simone de Beauvoir, *The Ethics of Ambiguity,* trans. Bernard Frechtman (Secaucus, NJ: Citadel Press, 1997 [1948]), part III, section 3.

17. Cherki, *Frantz Fanon,* 105.

18. Ibid.

19. Jeffrey S. Ahlman, "The Algerian Question in Nkrumah's Ghana, 1958–1960: Debating 'Violence' and 'Nonviolence' in African Decolonization," *Africa Today* 57, no. 2 (2010): 66–84.

20. Frantz Fanon, "This Africa to Come," in *Toward the African Revolution: Political Essays,* trans. Haakon Chevalier (New York: Grove, 1967 [1964]), 177–90.

21. Fanon, "West Indians and Africans," in *Toward the African Revolution,* 27.

22. Fanon, *The Wretched of the Earth,* trans. Farrington, 35, 36.

23. Ibid., 38, 40.

24. In his 2008 translation, Philcox often uses the terms "colonist" and "colonized subject." I am drawn to the earlier translations of "settler" and "native" due to their descriptive qualities specific to Algeria.

25. Fanon, *The Wretched of the Earth,* trans. Farrington, 41.

26. Frantz Fanon, *Black Skin, White Masks,* trans. Richard Philcox (New York: Grove Press, 2008 [1952]), xi.

27. Hussein Abdilahi Bulhan, *Frantz Fanon and the Psychology of Oppression* (New York: Plenum Press, 1985), 147–48; Cherki, *Frantz Fanon,* 16, 107–8; George Ciccariello-Maher, "To Lose Oneself in the Absolute: Revolutionary Subjectivity in Sorel and Fanon," *Human Architecture: Journal of the Sociology of Self-Knowledge* 5, no. 3 (2007): 101–11; Sartre, "Preface," in *The Wretched of the Earth,* trans. Philcox, xlix.

28. Fanon, *The Wretched of the Earth,* trans. Farrington, 94.

29. Ibid., 51, 52.

30. Ibid., 46–50.

31. Ibid., 60.

32. Ibid., 61.

33. Ibid., 62–69, 111. Fanon's approach has drawn criticism, with Pierre Bourdieu disparaging the idea of the peasantry as a "revolutionary class" given that it was "overwhelmed by the war, by the concentration camps, and by the mass deportations." Bourdieu was conscripted into the French army in 1955 to serve in Algeria and later did ethnographic work there during the war. See Le Sueur, *Uncivil War,* 252–54.

34. Fanon, *The Wretched of the Earth,* trans. Farrington, 40. On this issue and the black Marxist tradition, see Anthony Bogues, *Black Heretics, Black Prophets: Radical Political Intellectuals* (New York: Routledge, 2003), chapter 5.

35. Cherki, *Frantz Fanon,* 172.

36. Joel Beinin, *Workers and Peasants in the Modern Middle East* (New York: Cambridge University Press, 2001), 130.

37. Fanon, *The Wretched of the Earth,* trans. Farrington, 61.

38. Ibid., 69–71.

39. Ibid., 70.

40. Ibid., 75–83.

41. Fanon, *The Wretched of the Earth,* trans. Philcox, 23.

42. Fanon, *The Wretched of the Earth,* trans. Farrington, 84.

43. Ibid., 93.

44. Ibid., 102. It should be noted that the creation of the European Union occurred during the same period with the signing of the 1957 Treaty of Rome.

45. Ibid., 106.

46. For discussion of national consciousness and nationalism, see Jane Anna Gordon, *Creolizing Political Theory: Reading Rousseau through Fanon* (New York: Fordham University Press, 2014), chapter 4; Neil Lazarus, "Disavowing Decolonization: Fanon, Nationalism, and the Problematic of Representation in Current Theories of Colonial Discourse," *Research in African Literatures* 24, no. 4 (1993): 69–98. Aimé Césaire also considered the nation a problematic concept, though for different reasons. See Aimé Césaire, *Discourse on Colonialism,* trans. Joan Pinkham (New York: Monthly Review Press, 2000 [1955]), 74.

47. On this title translation, see Fanon, *The Wretched of the Earth,* trans. Farrington.

48. Ibid., 109–11.

49. Ibid., 113.

50. Ibid., 114.

51. Ibid., 129.

52. On this division, see Alistair Horne, *A Savage War of Peace: Algeria 1954–1962* (New York: The New York Review of Books, 2006), 142–43.

53. Fanon, *The Wretched of the Earth,* trans. Farrington, 136–37.

54. Ibid., 140–41.

55. Ibid., 139.

56. Ibid., 142–43.

57. Fanon, *The Wretched of the Earth,* trans. Philcox, 93.

58. Fanon, *The Wretched of the Earth,* trans. Farrington, 146.

59. Fanon, *The Wretched of the Earth,* trans. Philcox, 96.

60. Fanon, *The Wretched of the Earth,* trans. Farrington, 148–49. Philcox translates this chapter title as "The Trials and Tribulations of National Consciousness."

61. Ibid., 152, 158–59.

62. Fanon, *The Wretched of the Earth,* trans. Philcox, 106.

63. Fanon, *The Wretched of the Earth,* trans. Farrington, 165.

64. Macey, *Frantz Fanon,* 455, 458. On the negotiation process, see Matthew Connelly, *A Diplomatic Revolution: Algeria's Fight for Independence and the Origins of the Post–Cold War Era* (New York: Oxford University Press, 2002), chapter 9.

65. Fanon, *The Wretched of the Earth,* trans. Farrington, 169.

66. Ibid., 176.

67. Ibid., 193.

68. Ibid., 193, 200, 201.

69. Ibid., 203.

70. Ibid., 204–5.

71. Ibid., 206, 209. Fanon was present at the 1960 Afro-Asian People's Solidarity Conference hosted by Touré in Conakry.

72. Ibid., 236.

73. Ibid., 210.

74. Fanon, *The Wretched of the Earth,* trans. Philcox, 148. This citation of Songhai (or Songhay) civilization, which in itself challenges a Négritude vision of civilization, drew from his brief experience in Mali.

75. Ibid.

76. Ibid.

77. Fanon, *The Wretched of the Earth,* trans. Farrington, 225.

78. Ibid., 231. This view echoes arguments from Leon Trotsky, *Art and Revolution: Writings on Literature, Politics, and Culture,* ed. Paul N. Siegel (London: Pathfinder Press, 1970).

79. Fanon, *The Wretched of the Earth,* trans. Farrington, 231.

80. Ibid., 232.

81. Fanon, *The Wretched of the Earth,* trans. Philcox, 177.

82. Ibid., 178.

83. Ibid.

84. Fanon, *The Wretched of the Earth,* trans. Farrington, 247.

85. Ibid., 247–48. This "twofold" process also bears the trace of Marxist thought, since Marx, Lenin, and Trotsky used such terminology to describe the stages toward communist revolution.

86. Fanon, *The Wretched of the Earth,* trans. Philcox, 184.

87. Fanon, *The Wretched of the Earth,* trans. Farrington, 270.

88. Ibid., 253.

89. Fanon, *The Wretched of the Earth,* trans. Philcox, 233.

90. Barbara Harlow, "Narratives of Resistance," *New Formations* 1 (1987): 135.

91. This expansiveness shares affinities with Césaire, *Discourse on Colonialism,* 31–34.

92. Fanon, *The Wretched of the Earth,* trans. Philcox, 61.

93. Fanon, *The Wretched of the Earth,* trans. Farrington, 164.

94. Irene L. Gendzier, *Frantz Fanon: A Critical Study* (New York: Pantheon, 1973), 249–57.

95. Cherki, *Frantz Fanon,* 157; Nigel C. Gibson, "A Wholly Other Time? Fanon, the Revolutionary, and the Question of Organization," *South Atlantic Quarterly* 112, no. 1 (2013): 41–42.

96. On Marx, I paraphrase Walter Benjamin, *The Work of Art in the Age of Its Technological Reproducibility, and Other Writings on Media,* ed. Michael W. Jennings, Brigid Doherty, and Thomas Y. Levin (Cambridge, MA: Harvard University Press, 2008), 19.

97. Fanon, *The Wretched of the Earth,* trans. Farrington, 240.

98. Ibid., 37.

99. Ibid.

100. Ibid., 316. Fanon's notion of a "new man" echoes Marx's notion of a "total man."

101. Ibid., 314.

102. Ibid., 315.

103. Ibid.

**Conclusion. Transcending the Colonial Unconscious: Radical Empathy as Politics**

1. Frantz Fanon, *Black Skin, White Masks,* trans. Richard Philcox (New York: Grove, 2008 [1952]), 205.

2. David Macey, *Frantz Fanon: A Biography* (New York: Picador, 2000), 490–91.

3. Macey, *Frantz Fanon,* 394–95, 451–52, 457–58, 490. See also Matthew Connelly, *A Diplomatic Revolution: Algeria's Fight for Independence and the Origins of the Post–Cold War Era* (New York: Oxford University Press, 2002), 259–64.

4. Though his diplomatic role was significant, it could be interpreted as marginalizing him from the decision making of the FLN leadership.

5. Homi K. Bhabha, "Foreword: Framing Fanon," in Frantz Fanon, *The Wretched of the Earth,* trans. Richard Philcox (New York: Grove, 2004 [1961]), vii; Alice Cherki, *Frantz Fanon: A Portrait,* trans. Nadia Benabid (Ithaca, NY: Cornell University Press, 2006), 164–65.

6. Connelly, *A Diplomatic Revolution,* 265; Martin Evans, *Algeria: France's Undeclared War* (New York: Oxford University Press, 2012), 335.

7. Vincent Crapanzano, *The Harkis: The Wound That Never Heals* (Chicago: University of Chicago Press, 2011), 56; Evans, *Algeria,* 337.

8. Connelly, *A Diplomatic Revolution,* 267.

9. The lower figure is from Crapanzano, *The Harkis,* 105. The higher figure (estimated in 1964) is from Evans, *Algeria,* 341.

10. Connelly, *A Diplomatic Revolution,* 269–70. Some have argued that this bloodshed was a form of cathartic violence, thus vindicating Fanon. This perspective leaves open whether Fanon was morally justified in his rationales.

11. On continued maltreatment, see Crapanzano, *The Harkis,* 105. On diverse violence, see Evans, *Algeria,* 336.

12. Connelly, *A Diplomatic Revolution,* 290–92.

13. Ibid., 284.

14. On Fanon and the hard-liners, see Cherki, *Frantz Fanon,* 152.

15. Todd Shepard, *The Invention of Decolonization: The Algerian War and the Remaking of France* (Ithaca, NY: Cornell University Press, 2008), 272.

16. On postcolonial France, see James D. Le Sueur, "Beyond Decolonization? The Legacy of the Algerian Conflict and the Transformation of Identity in Contemporary France," *Historical Reflections/Réflexions Historiques* 28, no. 2 (2002): 277–91; Kristin Ross, *Fast Cars, Clean Bodies: Decolonization and the Reordering of French Culture* (Cambridge, MA: MIT Press, 1996); Joan Wallach Scott, *The Politics of the Veil* (Princeton, NJ: Princeton University Press, 2010); Dominic Thomas, *Africa and France: Postcolonial Cultures, Migration, and Racism* (Bloomington: Indiana University Press, 2013). On the decolonization of Europe, see Fanon, *The Wretched of the Earth,* lvii, 235–39.

17. Irene L. Gendzier, *Frantz Fanon: A Critical Study* (New York: Pantheon, 1973), 175–81.

18. The tensions between Ben Bella and Boumédiène can be attributed to differences that emerged between the exiled GPRA, with which Ben Bella was aligned, and the ALN's military struggle inside Algeria, with which Boumédiène was aligned. Boumédiène was sympathetic to Fanon's ideas. See ibid., 252–57.

19. Evans, *Algeria,* 340–42. On the tensions between Third Worldism and dependence, see Robert Malley, *The Call from Algeria: Third Worldism, Revolution, and the Turn to Islam* (Berkeley: University of California Press, 1996).

20. Cherki, *Frantz Fanon,* 172.

21. On Fanon's wish, see Cherki, *Frantz Fanon,* 166. On Fanon's family, see Joby Fanon, *Frantz Fanon, My Brother: Doctor, Playwright, Revolutionary,* trans. Daniel Nethery (Lanham, MD: Lexington Books, 2014 [2004]), 106.

22. Aimé Césaire, "Hommage à Frantz Fanon," *Présence africaine* 60 (1962): 131–34. Fanon was buried just across the border in 1961, and his body was moved to its current location in Aïn·Kerma in 1965. Macey, *Frantz Fanon,* 6.

23. Cherki, *Frantz Fanon,* 185; Gendzier, *Frantz Fanon,* 257.

24. On Josie Fanon, see the appendix in Christian Filostrat, *Negritude Agonistes, Assimilation against Nationalism in the French-Speaking Caribbean and Guyane* (Cherry Hill, NJ: Africana Homestead Legacy Publishers, 2008). On her elusiveness, see Fanon, *Frantz Fanon, My Brother,* viii. See also Assia Djebar, *Algerian White,* trans. David Kelley and Marjolijn de Jager (New York: Seven Stories Press, 2000), 91–92, 176.

25. On attention toward the English translation of his work, see Robert Coles, "Abused and Abusers," *New York Times,* April 30, 1967, 298. On the minimization of Fanon's memory by the Algerian government, see Gendzier, *Frantz Fanon,* 246.

26. Stokely Carmichael (Kwame Turé), *Stokely Speaks: From Black Power to Pan-Africanism* (Chicago: Chicago Review Press, 2007 [1971]).

27. Amílcar Cabral, "National Liberation and Culture," *Transition* 45 (1974): 12–17. See also Robert Blackey, "Fanon and Cabral: A Contrast in Theories of Revolution for Africa," *Journal of Modern African Studies* 12, no. 2 (1974): 191–209; Patrick Chabal, "The Social and Political Thought of Amílcar Cabral: A Reassessment," *Journal of Modern African Studies* 19, no. 1 (1981): 31–56; Firoze Manji and Bill Fletcher Jr., eds., *Claim No Easy Victories: The Legacy of Amilcar Cabral* (Dakar: CODESRIA, 2013).

28. Steve Biko, *I Write What I Like: Selected Writings* (Chicago: University of Chicago Press, 2002).

29. Ruth First, *The Barrel of a Gun: Political Power in Africa and the Coup d'État* (New York: Penguin, 1970).

30. Hamid Dabashi, *Theology of Discontent: The Ideological Foundation of the Islamic Revolution in Iran* (New York: New York University Press, 1993), 110–11; Ali Shari'ati, *Marxism and Other Western Fallacies: An Islamic Critique,* trans. R. Campbell (Berkeley, CA: Mizan Press, 1980).

31. Paul Gilroy, *Against Race: Imagining Political Culture beyond the Color Line* (Cambridge, MA: Harvard University Press, 2000); Mahmood Mamdani, *When Victims Become Killers: Colonialism, Nativism, and the Genocide in Rwanda* (Princeton, NJ: Princeton University Press, 2002).

32. For a similar point, see Neil Lazarus, *The Postcolonial Unconscious* (Cambridge: Cambridge University Press, 2011), 161.

33. David Scott, *Refashioning Futures: Criticism after Postcoloniality* (Princeton, NJ: Princeton University Press, 1999), 197. See also Anthony C. Alessandrini, *Frantz Fanon and the Future of Cultural Politics: Finding Something Different* (Lanham, MD: Lexington Books, 2014), chapter 1.

34. Frantz Fanon, *A Dying Colonialism,* trans. Haakon Chevalier (New York: Grove Press, 1965 [1959]), 26.

35. Nigel C. Gibson, *Fanon: The Postcolonial Imagination* (Cambridge: Polity, 2003), 10, 11.

36. Jean-Paul Sartre, *Being and Nothingness,* trans. Hazel E. Barnes (New York: Washington Square Press, 1992 [1943]), part one, chapter 2.

37. Hortense J. Spillers, *Black, White, and in Color: Essays on American Literature and Culture* (Chicago: University of Chicago Press, 2003), 383.

38. Fanon is cited in the essay "Reversion and Diversion" in Édouard Glissant, *Caribbean Discourse: Selected Essays,* trans. J. Michael Dash (Charlottesville: University of Virginia Press, 1999).

39. Gendzier, *Frantz Fanon,* 180.

40. Edward W. Said, "Travelling Theory Reconsidered," in *Rethinking Fanon: The Continuing Dialogue,* ed. Nigel C. Gibson (Amherst, NY: Humanity Books, 1999), 214.

41. Gibson, *Fanon,* 8, 10.

42. Nelson Maldonado-Torres, *Against War: Views from the Underside of Modernity* (Durham, NC: Duke University Press, 2008), chapter 4.

43. Fanon, *Black Skin, White Masks,* 24.

44. Ibid., 206.

45. Adolfo Gilly, "Introduction," in Fanon, *A Dying Colonialism,* 2.

46. Fanon, *A Dying Colonialism,* 26.

47. Nelson Mandela, *Long Walk to Freedom* (Boston: Little, Brown, 1994), 298.

48. Angela Y. Davis, *Women, Race, and Class* (New York: Random House, 1981); Gilroy, *Against Race;* Fred Moten, "The Case of Blackness," *Criticism* 50, no. 2 (2008): 177–218; Sylvia Wynter, "Unsettling the Coloniality of Being/Power/Truth/Freedom: Towards the Human, After Man, Its Overrepresentation—An Argument," *CR: The New Centennial Review* 3, no. 3 (2003): 257–337. For an overview (albeit an Anglocentric one), see Cedric J. Robinson, *Black Marxism: The Making of the Black Radical Tradition* (Chapel Hill: University of North Carolina Press, 2000 [1983]).

49. Fanon, *Black Skin, White Masks,* 206.

50. Nelson Mandela, "'I am prepared to die': Nelson Mandela's Statement from the Dock at the Opening of the Defence Case in the Rivonia Trial" found at: db.nelsonmandela.org/speeches.

51. My emphasis. Fanon, *The Wretched of the Earth,* 178.

52. For further discussion, see the introduction and conclusion to Christopher J. Lee, *Unreasonable Histories: Nativism, Multiracial Lives, and the Genealogical Imagination in British Africa* (Durham, NC: Duke University Press, 2014).

# Bibliography

**Works by Frantz Fanon (Recent Translations Only)**

Fanon, Frantz. *Black Skin, White Masks.* Translated by Richard Philcox. New York: Grove Press, 2008 [1952].
———. *A Dying Colonialism.* Translated by Haakon Chevalier. New York: Grove Press, 1965 [1959].
———. *Toward the African Revolution: Political Essays.* Translated by Haakon Chevalier. New York: Grove, 1967 [1964].
———. *The Wretched of the Earth.* Translated by Richard Philcox. New York: Grove, 2004 [1961].

**Select Recommendations for Further Reading**

Bhabha, Homi K. *The Location of Culture.* London: Routledge, 1994.
Biko, Steve. *I Write What I Like: Selected Writings.* Edited by Aelred Stubbs. Chicago: University of Chicago Press, 2002.
Bulhan, Hussein Abdilahi. *Frantz Fanon and the Psychology of Oppression.* New York: Plenum Press, 1985.
Camus, Albert. *Algerian Chronicles.* Edited by Alice Kaplan. Translated by Arthur Goldhammer. Cambridge, MA: Harvard University Press, 2013.
Césaire, Aimé. *Discourse on Colonialism.* Translated by Joan Pinkham. New York: Monthly Review Press, 2000 [1955].
———. *Notebook of a Return to the Native Land.* Edited by Annette Smith. Translated by Clayton Eshleman. Middletown, CT: Wesleyan University Press, 2001.

Césaire, Suzanne. *The Great Camouflage: Writings of Dissent (1941–1945)*. Edited by Daniel Maximin. Translated by Keith L. Walker. Middletown, CT: Wesleyan University Press, 2012.

Cherki, Alice. *Frantz Fanon: A Portrait*. Translated by Nadia Benabid. Ithaca, NY: Cornell University Press, 2006.

Connelly, Matthew. *A Diplomatic Revolution: Algeria's Fight for Independence and the Origins of the Post–Cold War Era*. New York: Oxford University Press, 2003.

Cooper, Frederick. *Citizenship between Empire and Nation: Remaking France and French Africa, 1945–1960*. Princeton, NJ: Princeton University Press, 2014.

Crapanzano, Vincent. *The Harkis: The Wound That Never Heals*. Chicago: University of Chicago Press, 2011.

Di-Capua, Yoav. "Arab Existentialism: An Invisible Chapter in the Intellectual History of Decolonization." *American Historical Review* 117, no. 4 (2012): 1061–91.

Dubois, Laurent. *Avengers of the New World: The Story of the Haitian Revolution*. Cambridge, MA: Harvard University Press, 2005.

Edwards, Brent Hayes. *The Practice of Diaspora: Literature, Translation, and the Rise of Black Internationalism*. Cambridge, MA: Harvard University Press, 2003.

Evans, Martin. *Algeria: France's Undeclared War*. New York: Oxford University Press, 2012.

Fanon, Joby. *Frantz Fanon, My Brother: Doctor, Playwright, Revolutionary*. Translated by Daniel Nethery. Lanham, MD: Lexington Books, 2014 [2004].

Gates, Henry Louis, Jr. "Critical Fanonism." *Critical Inquiry* 17, no. 3 (1991): 457–70.

Geismar, Peter. *Fanon*. New York: Dial Press, 1971.

Gendzier, Irene L. *Frantz Fanon: A Critical Study*. New York: Pantheon, 1973.

Gibson, Nigel C. *Fanon: The Postcolonial Imagination*. London: Polity, 2003.

———, ed. *Rethinking Fanon: The Continuing Dialogue*. Amherst, NY: Humanity Books, 1999.

Gilroy, Paul. *The Black Atlantic: Modernity and Double-Consciousness*. Cambridge, MA: Harvard University Press, 1993.

Glissant, Édouard. *Caribbean Discourse: Selected Essays*. Translated by J. Michael Dash. Charlottesville: University Press of Virginia, 1989.

Gordon, Lewis R. *Fanon and the Crisis of European Man: An Essay on Philosophy and the Human Sciences*. New York: Routledge, 1995.

Gordon, Lewis R., T. Denean Sharpley-Whiting, and Renée T. White, eds. *Fanon: A Critical Reader.* Oxford: Blackwell, 1996.

Horne, Alistair. *A Savage War of Peace: Algeria 1954–1962.* New York: The New York Review of Books, 2006 [1977].

James, C. L. R. *The Black Jacobins: Toussaint L'Ouverture and the San Domingo Revolution.* New York: Vintage, 1989 [1938].

JanMohamed, Abdul R. "The Economy of Manichean Allegory: The Function of Racial Difference in Colonialist Literature." *Critical Inquiry* 12, no. 1 (1985): 59–87.

Keller, Richard C. *Colonial Madness: Psychiatry in French North Africa.* Chicago: University of Chicago Press, 2007.

Le Sueur, James. *Uncivil War: Intellectuals and Identity Politics during the Decolonization of Algeria.* 2nd ed. Lincoln: University of Nebraska Press, 2005.

Macey, David. *Frantz Fanon: A Biography.* New York: Picador, 2000.

Maldonado-Torres, Nelson. *Against War: Views from the Underside of Modernity.* Durham, NC: Duke University Press, 2008.

Malley, Robert. *The Call from Algeria: Third Worldism, Revolution, and the Turn to Islam.* Berkeley: University of California Press, 1996.

Mannoni, Octave. *Prospero and Caliban: The Psychology of Colonization.* Translated by Pamela Powesland. New York: Praeger, 1956 [1950].

Marriott, David. "Whither Fanon?" *Textual Practice* 25, no. 1 (2011): 33–69.

McCulloch, Jock. *Black Soul, White Artifact: Fanon's Clinical Psychology and Social Theory.* Cambridge: Cambridge University Press, 1983.

Memmi, Albert. *The Colonizer and the Colonized.* Translated by Howard Greenfeld. Boston: Beacon Press, 1991 [1957].

———. "The Impossible Life of Frantz Fanon." *Massachusetts Review* 14, no. 1 (1973): 9–39.

Miller, Christopher L. *Nationalists and Nomads: Essays on Francophone African Literature and Culture.* Chicago: University of Chicago Press, 1998.

Moten, Fred. "The Case of Blackness." *Criticism* 50, no. 2 (2008): 177–218.

Peterson, Charles F. *Du Bois, Fanon, Cabral: The Margins of Elite Anti-Colonial Leadership.* Lanham, MD: Lexington Books, 2007.

Richardson, Michael, ed. *Refusal of the Shadow: Surrealism and the Caribbean.* Translated by Krzysztof Fijalkowski and Michael Richardson. London: Verso, 1996.

Robinson, Cedric. "The Appropriation of Frantz Fanon." *Race & Class* 35, no. 1 (1993): 79–91.

Scott, David. *Refashioning Futures: Criticism after Postcoloniality.* Princeton, NJ: Princeton University Press, 1999.

Sekyi-Otu, Ato. *Fanon's Dialectic of Experience.* Cambridge, MA: Harvard University Press, 1996.

Sharpley-Whiting, T. Denean. *Frantz Fanon: Conflicts and Feminisms.* Lanham, MD: Rowman & Littlefield, 1997.

Shepard, Todd. *The Invention of Decolonization: The Algerian War and the Remaking of France.* Ithaca, NY: Cornell University Press, 2008.

Vergès, Françoise. "Creole Skin, Black Mask: Fanon and Disavowal." *Critical Inquiry* 23, no. 3 (1997): 578–95.

Wilder, Gary. *Freedom Time: Negritude, Decolonization, and the Future of the World.* Durham, NC: Duke University Press, 2015.

Williams, Eric. *Capitalism and Slavery.* Chapel Hill: University of North Carolina Press, 1994 [1944].

Wynter, Sylvia. "Unsettling the Coloniality of Being/Power/Truth/Freedom: Towards the Human, After Man, Its Overrepresentation—An Argument." *CR: The New Centennial Review* 3, no. 3 (2003): 257–337.

# Index

Printed and bound by CPI Group (UK) Ltd, Croydon, CR0 4YY

09/06/2025

14685963-0001